CONCEPTS OF SPACE IN

TRADITIONAL INDIAN ARCHITECTURE

CONCEPTS OF SPACE IN TRADITIONAL INDIAN ARCHITECTURE

Yatin Pandya

Vastu-Shilpa Foundation
for Studies and Research in Environmental Design

Mapin Publishing

Reprint in 2023 by
Mapin Publishing Pvt. Ltd
706 Kaivanna, Panchvati, Ellisbridge
Ahmedabad 380006 INDIA
T: +91 79 40 228 228 • F: +91 79 40 228 201
E: mapin@mapinpub.com • www.mapinpub.com

Text and photographs by Yatin Pandya

Vastu-Shilpa Foundation for Studies and Research in Environmental Design
'Sangath', Thaltej Road,
Ahmedabad 380 054

ISBN: 978-81-89995-75-1

Edited by: Carmen Kagal
Design by: Jalp Lakhia / Mapin Design Studio
Draft layout: Pranali Parikh and Yatin Pandya
Separations: Reproscan, Mumbai
Printed at Thomson Press (India) Ltd.

Frontispiece: The different architectural elements and the varying intensity of light at the Adalaj Stepwell, near Ahmedabad, comprise an arresting ensemble of vignettes.

ACKNOWLEDGEMENTS

Unlocking and interpreting the numerous folds of existence in this land of immensity and extremities has been an intense journey through time and space, where many individuals, events and experiences have knowingly or unknowingly helped in reinforcing convictions and traversing the unknown–some by walking together, and some by confronting the path with questions.

While having been born in India has contributed by means of inheriting my ways of life and imbibing its subtleties, my journeys to other lands must have provided the neutral outlook to perceive the same objectively. Commitments towards teaching and academics may have forced one to question the fundamentals and not take things for granted, while the association with the Vastu-Shilpa Foundation gave the rigour and reason for the research.

The seeds of the enquiry were sown initially during the discussions for Pranali Parikh's undergraduate research dissertation on "Hindu Notions of Space Making". She has been associated with the project all along, since then, through phases of research, graphics as well as layout. Dilip Karpoor joined in, and his questioning and reasoning helped generate debate and conviction of ideas. His contribution has also extended to editing the text through numerous rounds and drafting the initial text on the spatial sequences of Ellora. Raajesh Moothan and Ashka Naik's help in the refinement of the final draft added finesse.

Pranali's miniature style drawing and architectural graphics, Smita Gupta and Ashka Naik's colour rendering of them as well as Priyamwada Singh's freehand sketches for the spatial sequences provided able visual support to the text. Stephan and Rolf took the initial steps towards digitising the drawings for Adalaj and Modhera. The Maharana Mewar Charitable Foundation Project Management Office provided the base drawings for the City Palace, Udaipur.

Joseph Verughese's help with typing, data organization as well as administrative aspects brought about the physicality of the document. Finally, it is only due to the total freedom of work environment at the Vastu-Shilpa Foundation and the unstinting support of Mr. Balkrishna Doshi that a casual enquiry blossomed into a formal study. This research has been undertaken at and is fully suported by the Vastu-Shilpa Foundation for Studies and Research in Environmental Design.

The journey continues, events keep unfolding, and I must thank Riddhi, my family and all others for travelling with me.

Yatin Pandya

CONTENTS

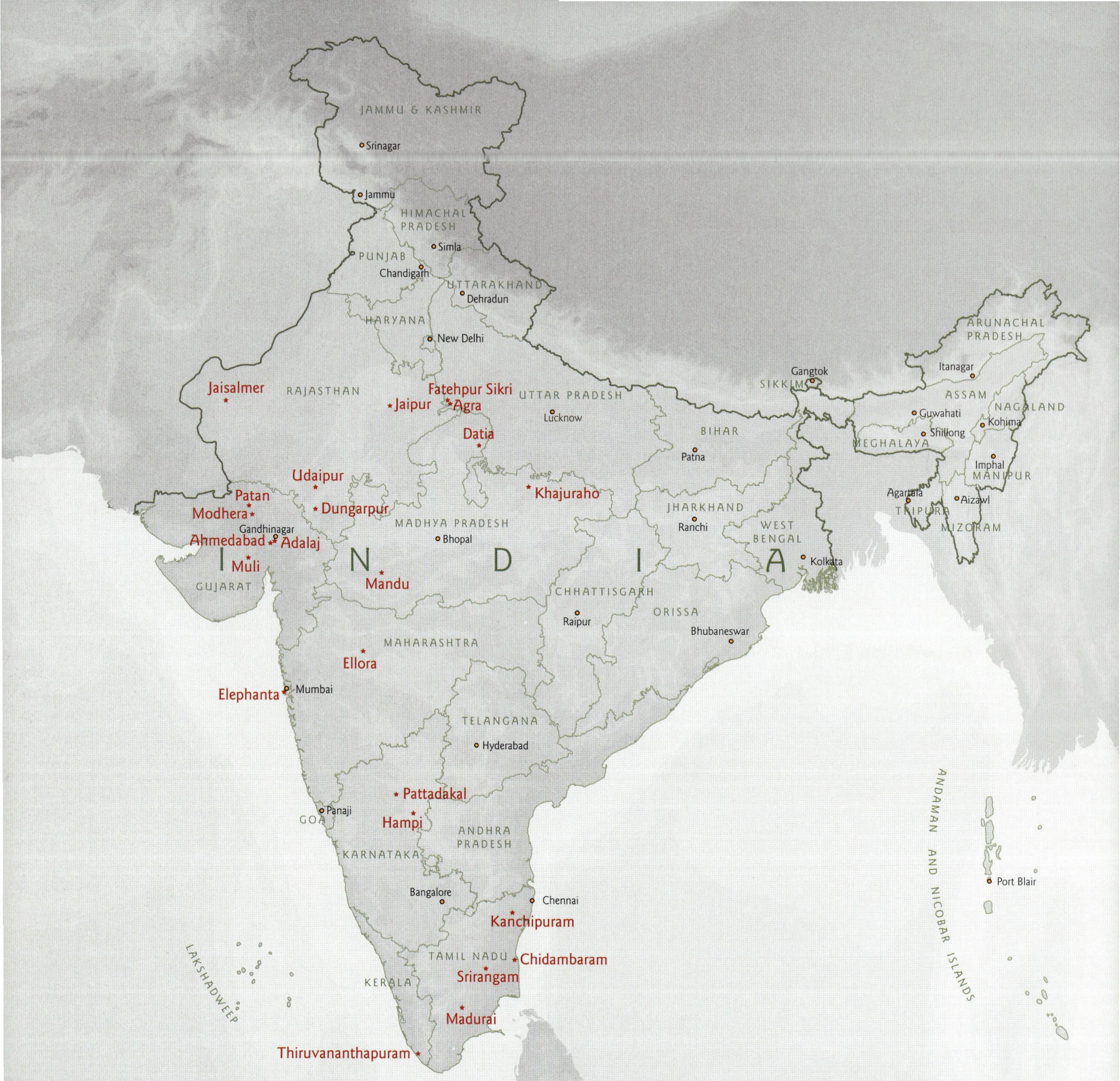

★ Places mentioned in the book

Based upon Survey of India maps with the permission of the Surveyor General of India.

PREFACE

What makes historic architecture awe-inspiring?

Why is it that even after centuries and millennia, despite functional obsolescence, these architectural masterpieces have retained their vitality?

What spatial qualities and organizational principles have rendered them timeless?

Can these qualities be deciphered and reinstated in contemporary times?

These questions become immensely pertinent in the Indian context due to its rich heritage and age-old traditions. In India, we live in three time zones simultaneously. The moorings of the past and aspirations for the future combine with the realities of the present, through an alchemy of conditioning over the millennia. Here, in India, the past continues as living tradition, both relevant and valid for the present.

The manifestation of an idea, architecture is a celebration of life. From philosophy and rituals to art forms and architecture, all are extensions of a way of life, echoing the underpinning notions of the Indian context. Any projections founded on the fundamental philosophical and ideological tenets of the place and people are therefore sustainable and timeless.

History is a function of time and space. Materials, construction techniques, style and 'isms' are conditioned by the context. Even form and scale are dividends of conditioned learning but the eventual experience is eternal, humanly universal and intuitive. Experiential richness and the ability to identify with pluralistic value systems are the hallmarks of timeless architecture. Traditional Indian architecture has ably demonstrated the universality of its communication as well as its validity within multiple value systems. This is achieved essentially by relying on spatial experiences derived through narratives–dynamic perception of space while in motion–its kinesthetics. The interactive process of encoding and decoding between the space and the perceiver orchestrates spatial narratives.

This research is an attempt at understanding the very roots of what constitutes the Indian context by examining its notions of time, space and existence. Deciphering their implications on the physically manifest, the study unravels the inherent virtues of traditional Indian architecture and interprets them as universal dictums, relevant to reinstate in contemporary times.

Yatin Pandya

INTERPRETATION

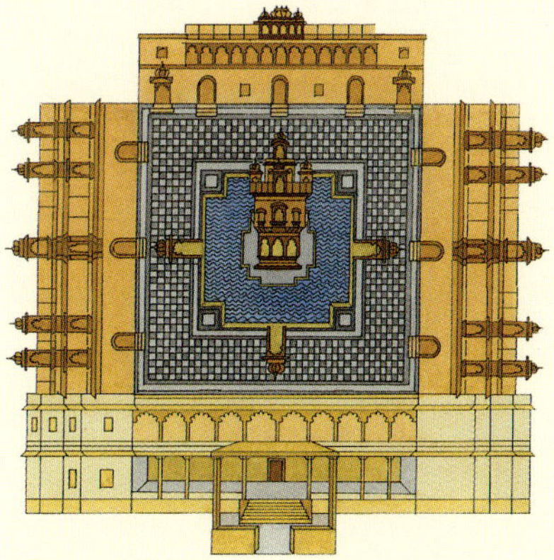

Spatial narratives in traditional Indian architecture–
An interpretation of a concept for contemporary relevance

History versus Tradition
Present as the Living Past

India! The land of antiquity. Its heritage is not confined to historic accounts of events and objects frozen in their own time and space, but is perpetuated as cultural and architectural traditions, which have transcended time and space to remain alive and appropriate even in the present. In India, history stays alive as living tradition. History and tradition both have their roots in the past, but history, for its inability to adapt to the changed time, is rendered obsolete as fossilized remains of a bygone era. Tradition, on the other hand, consistently adapts and suitably transforms to changed circumstances. This process of constant updation makes tradition survive and renders it timeless. It survived the past and promises to prevail in the future as it rests on collective concurrence, shared values and deep-rooted conditioning. Thus, tradition–as living heritage–retains its contemporariness and relevance even for the present times. In India, the people simultaneously live in three time zones. The legacies of the past and aspirations for the future effectively combine with the realities of the present.

1

2

3

4

1: Cultural associations and shared values keep monuments alive as living history, as at the Taj Mahal.

2: Tradition stays alive as the living past, as signified by a *tajia* procession during the Moharram festival.

3: Chimneys, historically the symbols of industrial prosperity but now obsolete in a changed time, lose their significance and are eliminated.

4: Traditionalism does not imply turning the clock backward. On the contrary, it is a progressive and consistent process of updation that subtly combines the 'old' with the 'new.' Seen here is a creative fusion of day-to-day utensils in the form of a deity, Ganesha.

Dynamics of Existence
The Alchemy of Time over Space

Time, in the Indian psyche, is a cyclic phenomenon. The faith in reincarnation, the cycle of birth, death and rebirth, the unending chain of construction, destruction and reconstruction, all reaffirm the belief in the recurrence of time. This assurance of recurrence instills a sense of equality as well as hope, much needed qualities in the pluralistic context with diverse value systems. However, although cyclic, time is not static. It is helical, evolving continuously. The concept of change is inexorably tied to the concept of time. The past and future are distinct domains in the continuum of time within which change occurs as a sequential series of events. The processes of evolution, involution and devolution go on constantly. What is of importance is that the progression is not as a linear continuity but as a helix or a spiral with a still centre and a dynamic periphery.

1: Nataraja, a classical form of the Lord Shiva immersed in *Tandava Nritya*, literally, the furious dance of destruction grieving the death of his wife Sati. It depicts a dynamic balance between creation, destruction and reconstruction, as symbolized here by the presence of the *damru*, a sort of drum, the ring of fire, the demon below, and the reassuring blessing open hand gesture respectively.

2: The cyclic notion of time is also evident in the ten incarnations of Lord Vishnu. This cycle is a helical path implying evolution due to investment in time.

3: Time through the ages has been conceptualized as a cyclic phenomenon. The Puranas, ancient scriptures, have personified time in the form of a Kalapurusha, whose form in itself symbolises its cyclic nature.

1

3▼ 2►

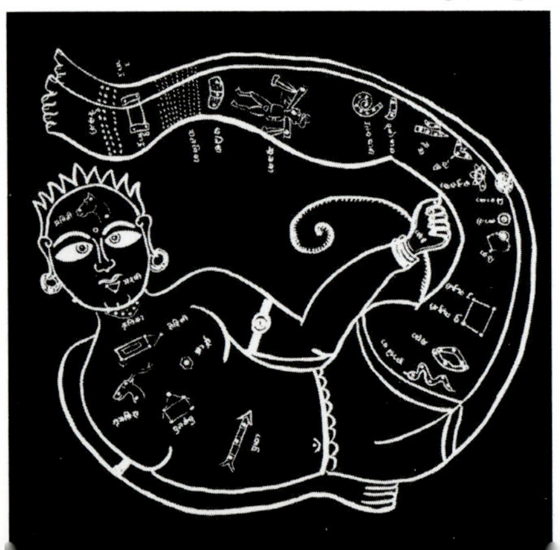

4

5

6

While time may recur, the alchemy of time with space renders the resolute always unique. For example, at any given time different spaces render themselves differently for an obvious reason–their physicality. Likewise the same physical space transforms drastically through its interaction with time. Therefore, having invested in time, the spaces change, rendering them vital, vibrant and dynamic. This constant juxtaposition of time over space is the essential premise of Indian architecture. This is a creative resolution under scarce resource conditions. A builtform, however complex, once realized, remains static. However, if made to interact with nature, the interface is always dynamic. The sun is not the same from morning to evening or from one season to another. Thus, direction, light intensity and shadow patterns changing all the time constantly redefine the builtform making it feel different and thereby alive. Thus, in the space-time chemistry, apart from the space dynamics, time also interacts actively to condition the mind and create a familiarity with the built object.

This aspect of time in architecture is introduced through structured movement. Movement exalts to become the key to spatial perception. Traditional Indian architecture is the story of movement and pauses where the kinesthetics of a space is fundamental to its experience and perception. The layering, movement corridors, thresholds and circumambulatory are aspects of this phenomenon in Indian architecture.

The diurnal metamorphosis of a traditional urban square, Manek Chowk, Ahmedabad, where spaces change radically over time: The square is a cow-grazing ground in the early mornings, where people collectively feed grass to the cattle. The same square becomes a platform for daily chores and is also used as a playground just before business hours. Through the day it converts into an intense business district with shops, hawkers, people and parking. Late evening through night, the square transforms into an outdoor eatery. Thus the same physical space is rendered different over time. This is an efficient optimization of space resources through the overlaid matrix of time.

4: Early morning–6:00 a.m. to 8:00 a.m.
5: Business hours–9:00 a.m. to 8:00 p.m.
6: Late evening–9:00 p.m. to 1:00 a.m.

Duality of Existence
World within a world

The Indian notion of existence rests on dualities. Atman, the infinitesmal building blocks of the human spirit, and Brahman, the overall schema of the universe, are the fundamental basis of any existence. This schema of dual existence simultaneously accepts the part as a whole and the whole as a part and gives rise to the concept of the 'world within a world.' Each entity is complete in itself at one plane and yet, at the other, is part of a larger system. A microcosm within a cosmos. This ensures freedom of individual expression, yet within the collective consensus. Of an identity within conformity. An effective tool to accommodate diversity while respecting the common bond of unity. This is critically required in a pluralistic society with multiple value systems. Individual belief systems must be accommodated, while the common code of understanding also needs to be maintained. This balance is finely arrived at through this notion of centres and sub-centres. Courtyards creating a world within a world and the schema of structure and infill, which bring out subtle variations within unified expressions, are obvious translations of these notions in architecture.
The courtyard is a characteristic device of Indian architecture that is most effective in creating a world within a world. The courtyard surrounded by the built mass creates an introverted response. Becoming a focus in itself, it allows for activities to spill into it and thrive without being disturbed by external conditions.

This element has been effectively used in designing royal campuses, palaces or even residences with different activities conforming to functions in multiple courtyards, where varying privacy gradients are respected in the form of a clearly delineated hierarchy of courts.

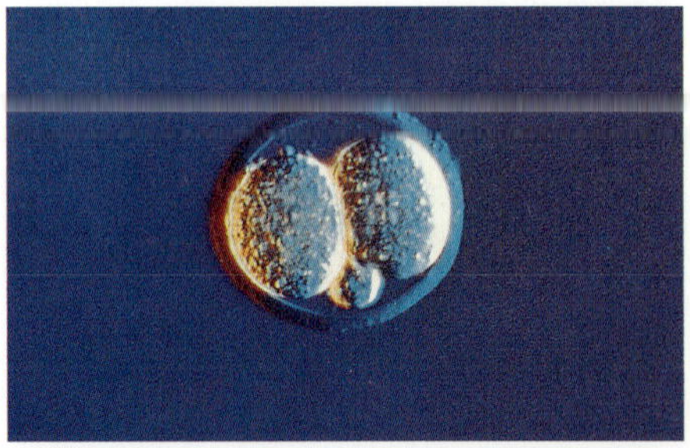

1

2

3▼

1: A biological cell, like an atom, believed to be the building block of the body, is still a complex, complete entity in itself.

2: India has a pantheon of around 330 million gods. This concept of many gods accepts the notion of many truths, each right for its believer, rather than a dictatorial structure that imposes a single truth. An effective concept to nurture the diverse notions of a pluralistic society.

3: A miniature style painting depicts the *Ras-lila*, a dance form adoring Lord Krishna, where each *gopi*, a devotee of the Lord, is under the illusion that she is dancing with him. Each one reaches out to the ultimate centre through one's own locus.
Source courtesy: Amit Ambalal

4: Contained yet open to nature, courtyards are a complete world in themselves supporting varied forms of human activity. A *haveli* or large residential mansion at Muli, Gujarat.

5: The 'world within a world' concept is manifested through yet another typology with a non-centric approach as seen in the Jagnivas Palace in Udaipur. Here courtyards are interlinked by corridors to form a flexible structure and each courtyard retains its individuality through its own scale and shape, yet complementing the overall schema of the space organization.

6: The Udai Bilas palace at Dungarpur creates different moods through its multiple court structure such as the vegetated garden-like forecourt, harem court with free-standing mirrored pavilion and the sacred innermost court with a shrine. A miniature painting style impression.

7: The Ranganatha Temple in the temple-town of Srirangam, in southern India, quite aptly demonstrates the concept of a 'world within a world' through concentric layering of walls and gates, where each subsequent layer gets more and more secured, sacred and withdrawn from worldly affairs, thus achieving a gradual transition from the corporeal to the celestial.

4

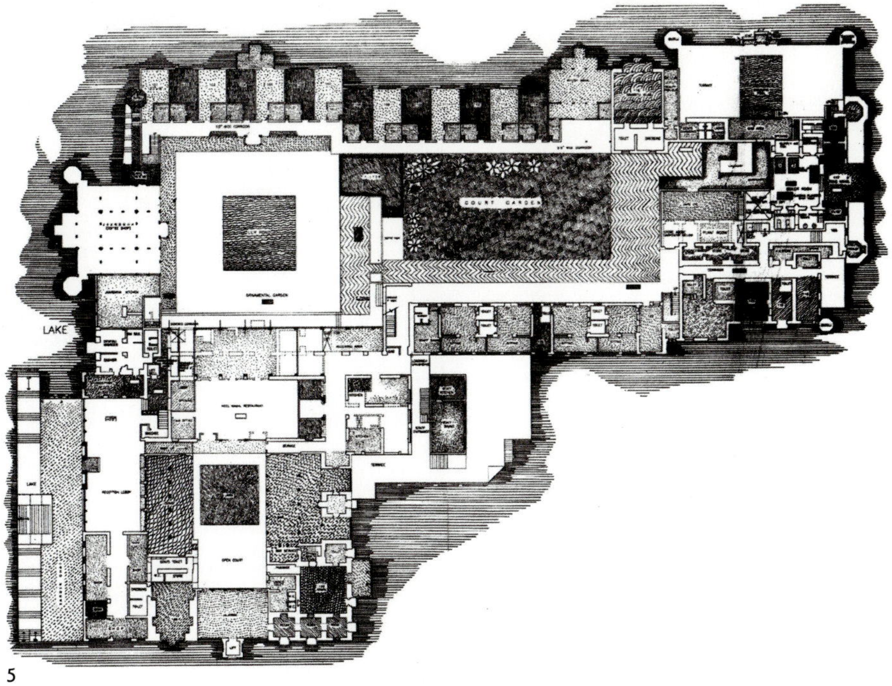

5

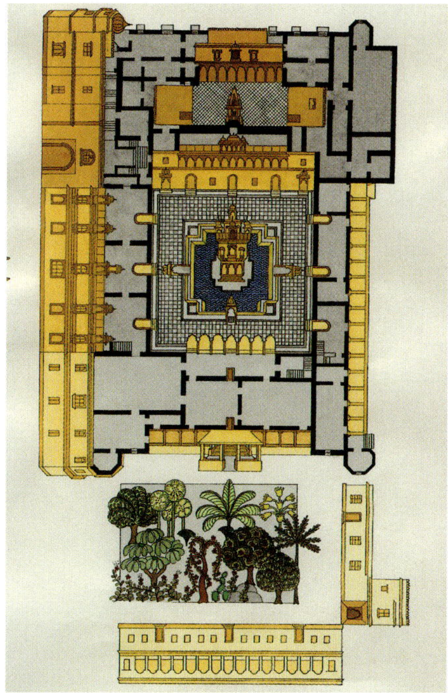

6

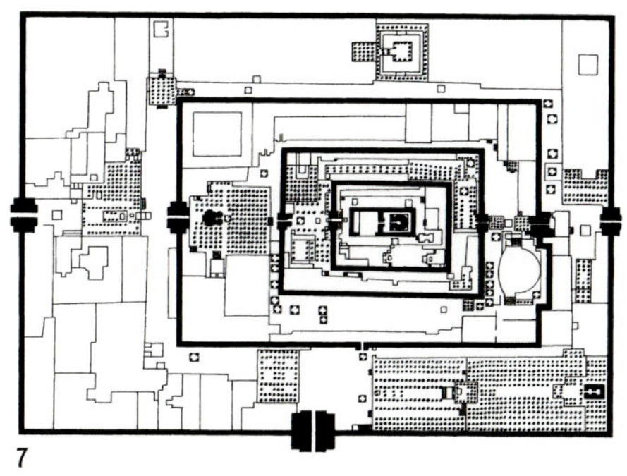

7

Duality of Existence
Part as a whole and the whole as a part

Understanding and acceptance of the duality of existence, where the part-to-whole relationship is not a hierarchical structure but a symbiotic one, gives in the overall schema of existence each component and each ingredient under it the freedom to exist, function as well as express itself independently. The collective resolution, however, still remains a chemistry of all the sub-components.

The same is expected of architecture. Streets of traditional towns best demonstrate this phenomenon. Streets get defined as a singular entity unified through zoning of fenestration, contiguity of the built edge as well as overall co-ordination of mass and scale. However, within this uniformity, identity is also respected and individuality is subtly expressed through freedom of choice, stylized elements, colours or innumerable gestures of personalization. These also help induce a sense of belonging without disrupting the overall harmony. The variation resultant of these inherent processes also helps break monotony and instill the overall with a rich sense of diversity.

1

2

3

1: Each individual is distinctly identifiable yet is a member of a clan, the society.

2: In Indian cuisine, a number of spices contribute to create a composite *rasa*, the resolute experience of taste. The absence of any one ingredient is readily perceptible, yet the composite essence is what matters.

3: *Thali*—the Indian food platter—as a phenomenon of combination meal epitomises Indian pluralism. It has pre-cooked, standardised, may be often mass-produced ingredients, even served the same way to all. But as a combination meal, it offers choices for permutation and combination. This makes each bite a unique experience. This also renders the *thali* as a personalised and unique experience as one is an active participant of the process. Two persons eating the same *thali*, despite the sameness of ingredients, do not share the same experience because the permutations, sequence and proportion remain unique to each person.

4: In Jaisalmer, identity within conformity is achieved by varied permutations and combinations of nearly modular elements, with continuity of built mass and harmony of scales.
Photo courtesy: Vikram Bhatt

5: At Jaipur, the arcades and continuous built mass act as binding factors, while the variety of openings and extensions provide variations.

6: *Pols*, the residential precincts of the traditional quarter of Ahmedabad, exhibit homogeneous heterogeneity through contiguous transition zones consisting of plinths, columns, *jharokhas* or balconies and *chhajas* or overhangs.

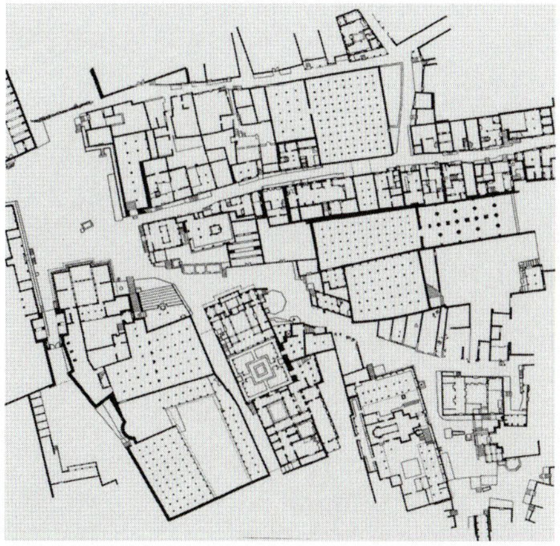

4

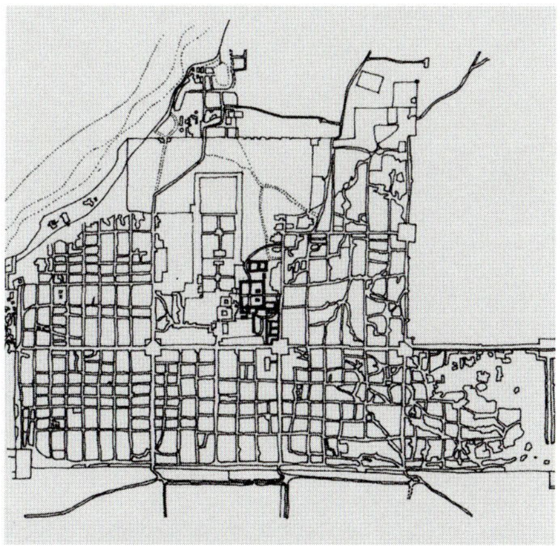

5

6

Bipolarity of existence
Opposites as counterpoints

The aspect of counterpoints is built into the Indian notion of existence as bipolar, where opposites reinforce each other. May it be *purusha* (man) and *prakriti* (nature), light and darkness, or solid and void, they are the mutually defining aspects. One shapes and gives validity to the existence of the other. Hence, apparent extremes co-exist in India. As counterpoints they become mutual references and an integral part of a self-balancing system ensuring continuum and endurance. This form of lateral understanding thus allows for apparent opposites to co-exist.

Opposites in the Indian context are exemplified and portrayed through various means, but can be broadly typified into three categories. Definition through negation where mutual definition is achieved through absolute negation, of one while the other is presented in full glory followed immediately by a reversal of roles. A co-existence of extremes, where one can be experienced only due to the presence of the other and vice versa. Relative identity, where once the two opposites are understood and identified they are placed within a particular relation as a composition which, due to their relative nature, becomes a third entity not characterising either but with the collective import of both.

1

3

4

2

1: Ardhanarishwara, a Chola bronze depicting Lord Shiva in his androgynous form. A personification of the synergy of opposites dissolving and fusing into itself the characteristic features of the two lateral physiognomies. Existence lies between the two extremes. Courtesy: Government Museum, Chennai

2: Relative Identity/Co-existance of extremes/Defined through negation.

3: The Shiv-linga, a metaphorical depiction of Lord Shiva, is symbolized through the union of the male and the female genitals, the union of the *purusha* (male) and the *prakriti* (primeval matter identified with the female principle) bringing forth life and existence.

4: *Arghya*, the ritual of offering water to the sun, brings together the opposites in the palm through reflection. Fire and water, ether and earth, warm and cool–which in reality remain apart–all come together notionally.

The aspect of existence by negation is best exemplified in traditional Indian architecture through symbiosis of the built with the unbuilt masses. Indian architecture often is the architecture of the unbuilt. The unbuilt is defined by the built while the built subsists through the unbuilt. The courtyard again is a key element in this regard. Culturally and climatically relevant, the activities extend into the enclosed area almost as outdoor rooms. Streets and courts are therefore the successful theatres of spontaneous activities.

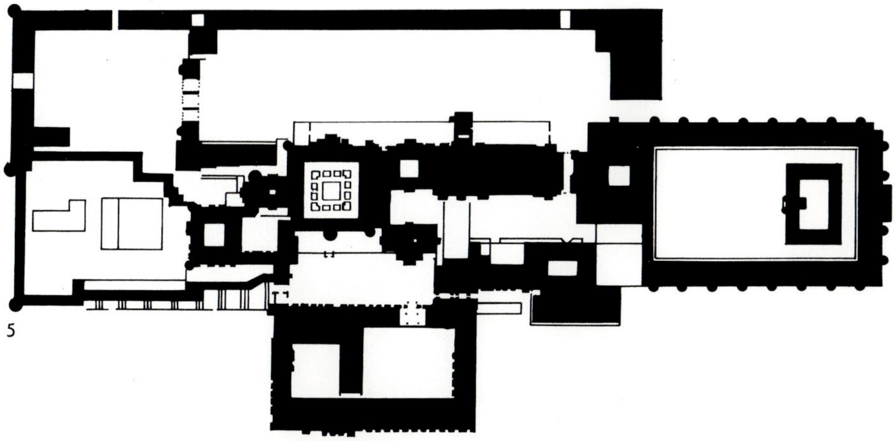

5

Cave temples are another apt example of this phenomenon of bipolar existence. The darkness of the cave helps appreciation of even a little source of light through courts, cracks and crevices. Caves also exhibit the coexistence of the raw with the finished–unfinished faces of the rock give meaning to the carved components. Juxtapositions of scooped-out spaces with the free-standing assembly also help substantiate each other mutually. The light crevices in cave temples, the court as a void within built-mass, water-bodies to reflect the sky, finished elements amidst raw surfaces, etc., are the juxtapositions in architecture reinforcing the sense of duality. Paradoxes prevail here, since, to an Indian psyche, notions rather than physical realities are more critical. 'Space' is a notional phenomenon, which shapes as well as exists by the context. Space-making is the sum total of the combination of time and space.

6

7

8

5: The City Palace, Udaipur, is a composition of built masses and voids where both proactively communicate with each other, contributing to the overall effect. Mass is registered due to the presence of void, while void is defined through mass.

6: Plasticity, roughness and monolithic masses are contrastingly juxtaposed with rectilinear, richly-carved columns at the cave temples as mutually referential.

7: Columns define the intercolumnation while the light does the shadow. The converse is as true.

8: Light gains meaning by its absence–cave temples, Ellora.

Spatial narratives

Sensorial, experiential and associational perception

Architecture is a celebration of life. The manifestation of an idea, it encodes messages and emotes feelings. Architecture communicates through spatial tools, whether they be the space sequences and their organization; elements of space-making and their scale and form; or the symbolism of surface articulation. It is this aspect of encoding and decoding that sets off an instantaneous dialogue between the user and the architectural product. The effectivity of the communication depends as much on the easy comprehension of the encoded messages as their appropriate compliance in builtform.

Communication takes place at three levels–sensorial, experiential and associational. Sensorial perception refers primarily to the physiological comforts accrued from physical resolution, essentially in response to environmental control. This bodily perception is humanly universal. The experiential aspect of communication is also universal, but the perception through this experience differs vastly as this aspect deals critically with the mental and emotional status of the perceiver. The process is spontaneous and reactionary to the nuances of space configuration and its dictates. The associational communication is a locale-specific perception requiring pre-conditioning and familiarity with the context or the acquired information base. It creates spiritual bonds and succeeds through in-depth understanding of cultural connotations. The complete communication occurs through a wholesome balance of all three.

In architecture, vision is the primary sense of perception. The inferred messages through perceived visual frames can guide and dictate behaviour. For example, a static, blank wall, with a curvature or inclination may guide the movement and, placed *en-face* as a baffle, may restrict it. This same wall, when overlaid with motifs and symbols, communicates further through associations that they may conjure. Such is the process of communication, where messages are encoded and decoded through an interactive visual process.

Architectural spaces can potentially nourish both emotionally and spiritually. A typical Hindu temple best illustrates this phenomenon. In the Hindu notion the act of prayer is very personal and a one-to-one connection is sought between the devotee and the deity. In order to facilitate such a notion the architecture of the temple must be complementary. In a temple, the sequence of *gopurams* (entrance gates), the series of ascending steps and platforms, the rising volumes of domes and *shikharas* or steeples, the increasing degree of enclosure, and the transition from the semi-open, multi-directional pavilions to the uni-directional dark sanctum enclosed by solid walls, all heighten the progression from the corporeal to the spiritual as one progresses from the *gopuram* to the *garbhagriha* or sanctum. This sense of transcendence from the worldly to the meta-physical, from the terrestrial to the celestial, from the matter to the mind is further enhanced by the culmination of the horizontal planes of the platform into a vertical axis through tall pointed *shikharas* symbolically reaching towards the heavens. In this manner, the elements of a building, its scale, size, volume, degrees of enclosure, levels of illumination as well as its motifs and decorations instill and evoke in the observer the ethos appropriate to the place.

Transcending time and space, good architecture remains communicative and interactive all the while through its spatial qualities. These spaces possess the qualities which establish a rapport with the perceivers and condition their perception even independent of their cultural backgrounds.

Timeless, ever-pervading architecture relies more on the fundamental attributes of space-making, ranging from approach and movement, scale and proportion, quality of light and shade to the relationship of the built with the unbuilt. These aspects are mostly qualitative and sometimes subjectively relative. Such archi-tecture therefore needs to be understood and interpreted through perceptual and experiential qualities and not by the abstractions of the plan geometry or static compositions of the facade elevations.

The visual dynamics of moving through the space and sensory perception of it is vital to wholesome architecture.

Kinesthetics, kinetic aesthetics, the dynamic perception of space through movement with ever-changing points of view and the varying vignettes resultant of the spatial composition, is the most fundamental facet of space-making in traditional Indian architecture. Time and again, the design of architectural masterpieces across the country, regardless of style, function or type, have been determined by this aspect of encoding narratives into their space organization, actively involving the perceiver, through the decoding process, in his journey through the space.

Space is conceived and perceived on the basis of movement through it. The journey, the process of moving through the space, in itself becomes the event. The clues for movement, inherent to the space, are revealed sequentially. The time gap required for the deconditioning of the previous and the preconditioning for the next is taken care of within the dimensions of the current space. This gradual unfolding of spaces creates a sense of curiosity within the visitor and involves them in the process.

Though the disposition of spaces is along the visual axis, the physical path of movement shifts to make the onlooker move around the notional centres of the space. Change in direction and diversion of movement cause variations in path and axis. Thus, axiality is characterized by variety. The whole length of the imperceptible axis is not revealed at once but is experienced as an episodic sequence of spaces. These sequences are deregularized by thresholds or pause elements. These elements not only create individual nodes of interest and enhance the pause in movement, but they also define spatial boundaries and reinforce the transition from one space to the other.

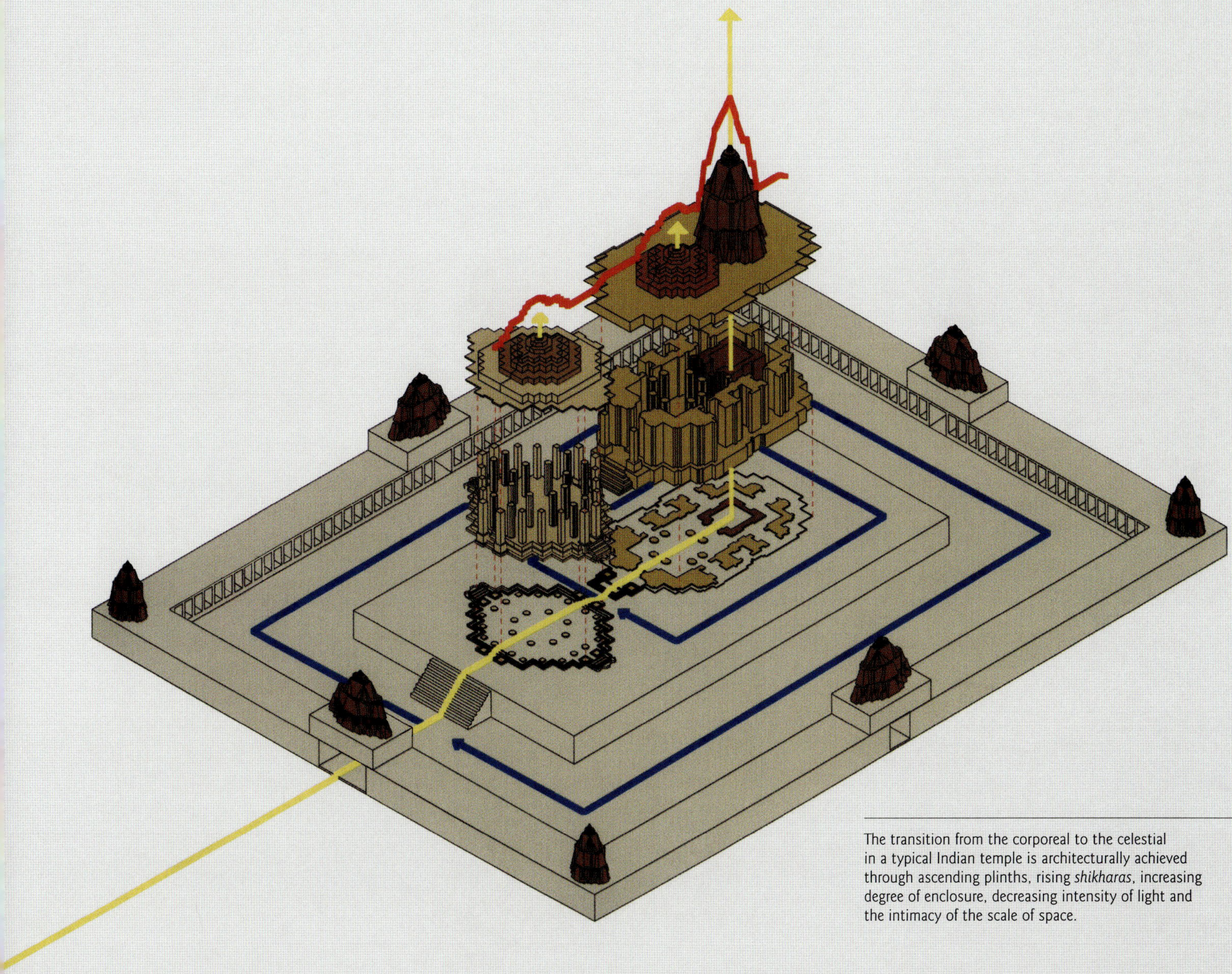

The transition from the corporeal to the celestial in a typical Indian temple is architecturally achieved through ascending plinths, rising *shikharas*, increasing degree of enclosure, decreasing intensity of light and the intimacy of the scale of space.

Kinesthetics in Meenakshi Sundareshwara Temple, Madurai, 15th–18th Centuries

The temple complex of Madurai, built over phases, ably demonstrates such narratives within the space and takes the perceiver through the process of visual interactive communication. The *gopuram*–a tall entrance gateway–provides the visual reference from faraway distances. It acts as a magnet, arresting the vision and attracting one towards it. It conjures a notion of having entered the religious realm. Thus guided by the *gopuram*, when one enters the gate, the subsequent layers of walls take over. The baffles in the form of wall planes and sculptural masses guiding one around these structures deflect the direct path of movement. The ritualistic circumambulation unassumingly becomes part of the movement. Each turn orients one to the shrines of sub-deities. A series of such foci and a sequence of colonnades slowly withdraws one from the corporal world and ushers him into the spiritual one. In this transition, the open colonnades gradually get more and more enclosed with increased presence of wall planes, as the sense of enclosure increases through the *sabha (nritya) mandapa*–pavilion for gatherings and dance–and the *goodha mandapa*–an antechamber to the deity's sanctum. The intensity of light inversely decreases and becomes nearly negligible at the fully enclosed *garbhagriha* or sanctum. This is a dark space ideally occupied only by the deity and the devotee. The stone sculpture of the deity is revered as God.

Here notion plays a more important role than the physical manifestation of the entity. Form loses value and association is revered as the darkness renders nearly imperceptible the actual form of the idol and thereby suggests its inconsequentiality. It instead allows for concentration of the mind, where the notions come through. Motifs and sculptures along the movement corridor also condition the mind while they too transform with increasing penetration into the precinct through depictions of royal stories to that of nymphs and *apsaras* (heavenly damsels) to gods and goddesses. Each baffle creates a pause to discover and reorient. The next set of clues gets unfolded at every subsequent pause, creating a sequential unfolding and a sense of discovery. This extended movement, adding the element of time over space, helps in the conditioning of the mind. This makes the journey both physically and mentally engaging and, thus, fulfilling.

1: A miniature style painting of the Meenakshi Temple at Madurai, fusing the plans, elevations and the movement paths.

2: Overall view of the Meenakshi Temple complex, where uni-centred but hierarchical, multi-layered organization with multiple linkages offers choices of paths to eventually culminate at the same core.

3: The towering *gopurams*–entrance gateways–as visual references and guiding magnets, attract movement towards entrances.

4: Decreasing light, increasing enclosure and intensifying iconography en route to the sanctum induce withdrawal from the external world.

5: Long corridors with larger than life depictions of grotesques, nymphs, gods and goddesses gradually become darker with the ultimate focus brightly lit at the end. These guide the mind and the movement.

6: In the dark sanctum, in the absence of all sensory stimuli, the intuitive faculties overtake conditioned learning, allowing for an intimate one-to-one dialogue.

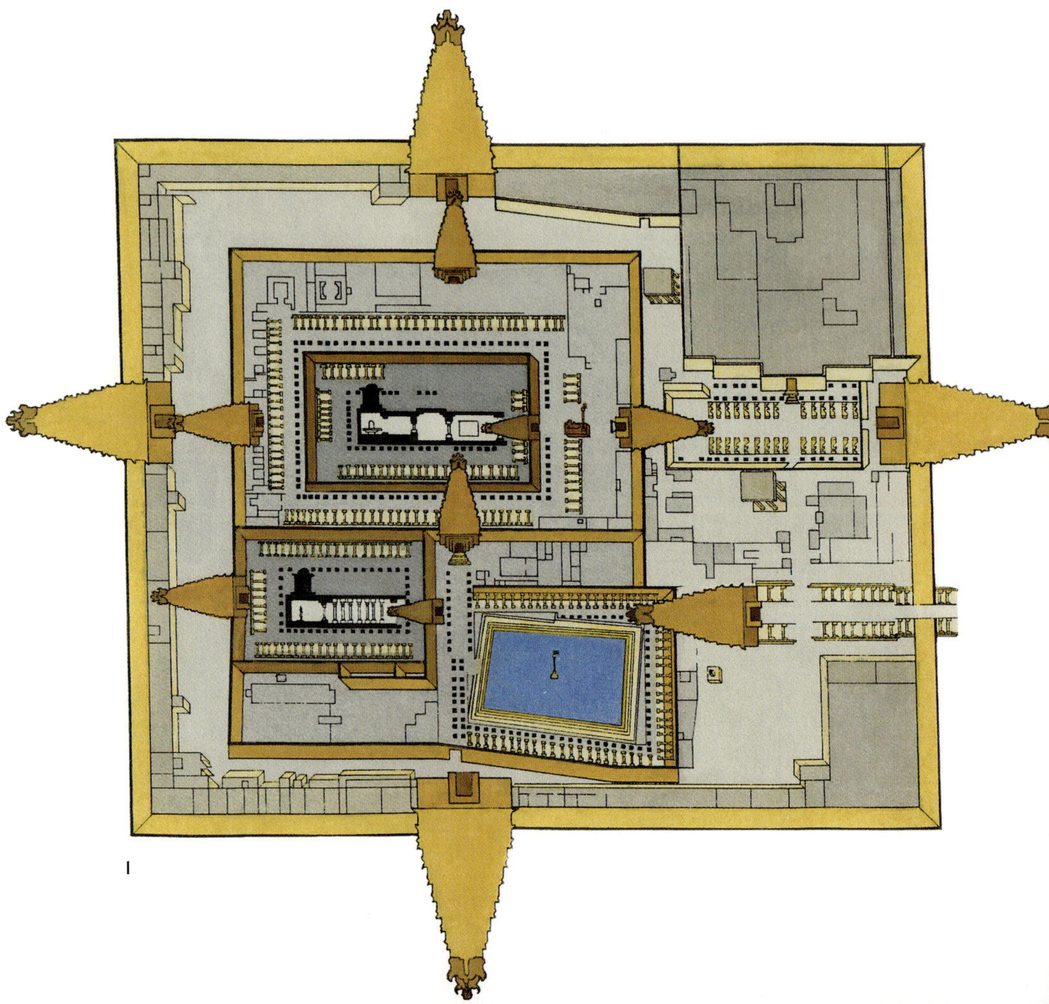

1

2

3

6

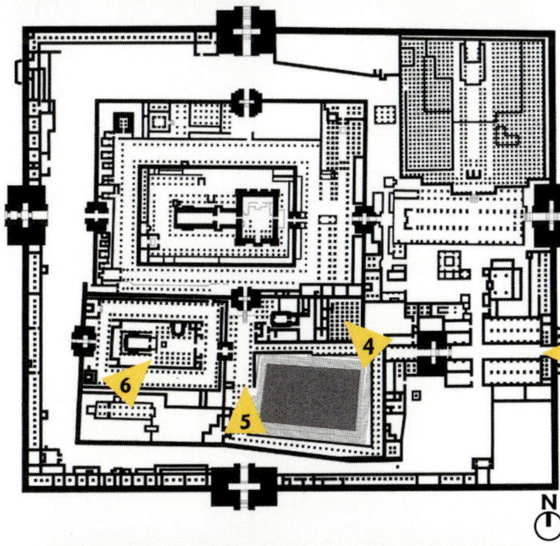

◄ 5

4

Kinesthetics in Hutheesing Jain Temple, Ahmedabad, 19th Century

The Hutheesing Jain Temple in Ahmedabad creates a spatial sequence attaining a one-to-one dialogue with the divine through shifting movement axes and a gradual morphing of spaces. The architectural resolution helps in such a conditioning through the spatial organization and juxtaposition of space-making elements. At Hutheesing Temple, the victory tower becomes the first visual reference and the focus from a distance. The next sequence of spaces begins from the extended, axially aligned entrance pavilion with ascending steps, a gateway and the first floor mass. The entrance gateway brings one *en-face* the main shrine, but this is where the circumambulatory takes over. A colonnade creates the peripheral ambulatory passage. Niches for idols of the *tirthankaras*, the 24 sanctified saints of Jainism whose presence throughout the journey start conditioning the mind, punctuate each inter-columnation. The more important of these have been specifically highlighted with bigger cella. These punctuations in the continuous path are also reflected in the enhanced flooring pattern, change in column rhythm and heightened *shikhara* size at cardinal points. These help in establishing pauses and cross-references to the main shrine to which they align.
After circumambulation, the journey further is axial, where the ascending steps, rising *shikhara* profiles, decreasing intensity of light aided by religious sculptures help create a gradual sense of withdrawal from the corporeal world. The passage here also passes through the three stage filters of the *sabha-mandapa*, *goodha-mandapa* and the *garbhagriha*. The Hutheesing Temple, thus, is yet another glorious example of movement guiding perception and exalting the physical journey into a personal intuitive experience.

1

1: Circumambulatory at Hutheesing Jain Temple for conditioning of mind and gradually orienting towards the cella.

2

3

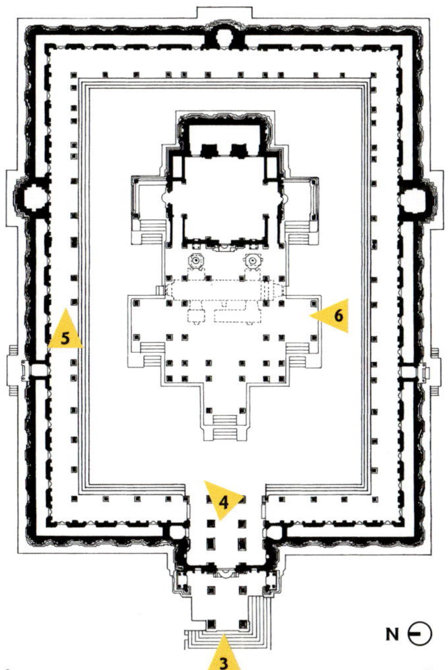

4

6

5 ▶

2: The victory tower assumes the visual identity as the landmark from a distance.

3: Contrasted against the blank peripheral wall, the intricately carved projecting portico defines the entrance, inviting movement.

4: The colonnade with *tirthankara* niches all along the circumambulatory initiates the visitor into the sacred realm.

5: Pauses along the movement path are punctuated through pronounced *shikhara* profiles, changing rhythm of columns as well as accentuated flooring patterns.

6: Ascending plinths, confinement and darkness gradually transcend to the cosmic.

Narratives through notions
Perceived Reality versus Physical Reality

Beginning from overall spatial organization to symbolic representation, narratives are creatively fused into the schema of Indian architecture through a number of devices. Primary amongst these is the usage of optical illusions and visual imagery. As interpreted by the Canadian architect Ron Lane-Smith, the entire proportioning system of ancient Indian architecture has been founded on the principles of visual coordination and perception at the human eye level. Perception from this specific level gives rise to unusual visual frames and compositions, imperceptible otherwise, created by perspectival alignments. The early cave temples creatively derive proportions and pauses putting into effect the principles of visual perception at the human eye level and using the visual axis at different points to bring out or hide selectively as one moves through. Such an exploration of space also discovers the juxtaposition of architectural elements to highlight prioritised visual compositions, creating optical illusions, revealing newer dimensions and connecting otherwise apparently unrelated and visually separated elements to act as significant foci, thus making the entire journey eventful.

This phenomenon of juxtaposition of visual frames is well demonstrated in the cave temples of Ellora. For example, in Cave 15, the door jamb into the court pavilion has niches near the top. Across, around 20 metres away, on the community quarter side at the upper level at each end, beside an apparent balcony projection are two angularly placed figures of

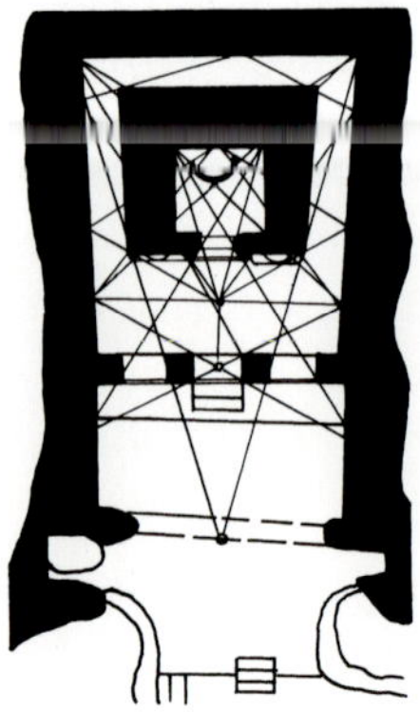

1

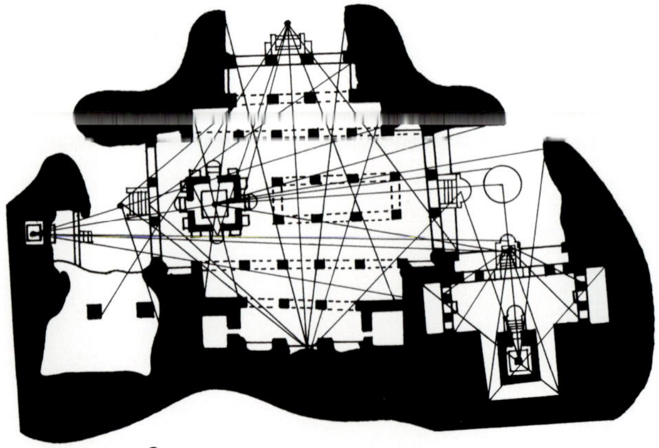

2

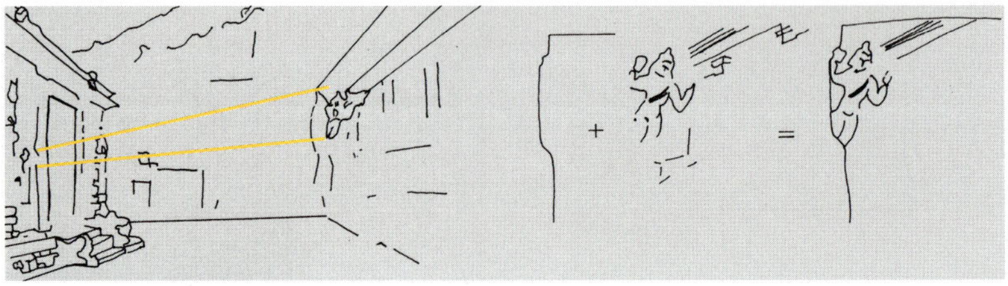

3

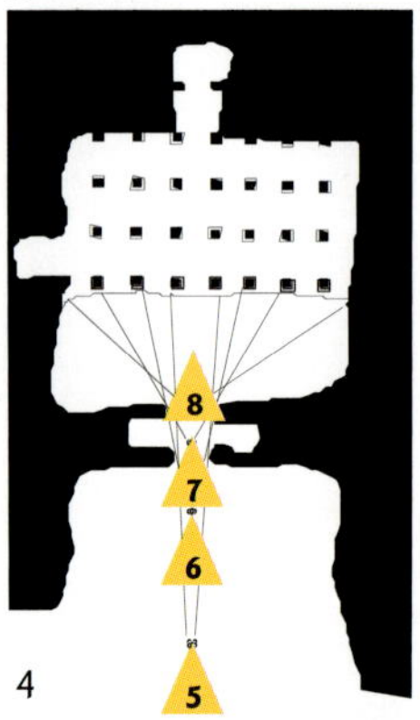

4

Caves from Ellora and Aurangabad illustrate how visual alignments become the actual proportioning tool.

1: Cave 2, Aurangabad.

2: Great Shiva Temple, Elephanta.

3: Sculpture on wall at Ellora Cave 15 visually coincides with the jamb niche 20 metres apart appearing as a bracket.

4: Key plan of the cave at Ellora indicating the view positions.

5, 6, 7 and 8: Visual frames which continually play with the scales and senses as one progresses along the edifice at Ellora.
Photo courtesy: Dilip Karpoor

5

6

7

8

superhuman entities. When one is just about to exit the *mandapa*, pavilion, the two gigantic figures across just fit into the niches. The juxtaposition makes them appear conjoined, providing architectural continuity across the intervening vista and giving a combined impression with the column bracket at the doorway. This creates a new imagery with a composite visual frame, giving added significance to the ensemble. The niche in the column capital exactly coincides with an inclined female figure on the wall across to give a combined expression with the column bracket at the doorway. These vignette compositions are used at times for visual scaling effects as well. As seen in the caves of Ellora, the sequential frames transform the vertical scales to horizontal expanses. In the first frame, from a distance, the overall scheme is perceived, not in totality but with concealment of portions of it. Here the scales are relative and do not refer to the human being. The next frame, perceived on approaching the building along the axis, is of vertical proportions revealing only the height of the structure–a part of the whole. The frame seen from the centre of the constricted entry begins to expand horizontally and on entering the court, exposes the entire scheme, a horizontal expanse totally dwarfing the height of the structure.

These principles are effectively applied to landscape elements also. One such profoundly successful application is in the placement of the water body for *vaju*–ablution in mosques. The water of the tank reflects the crown of the dome, but its image in totality is glimpsed only at the point of squatting down for the ritual washing. This is a subtle narrative yet a profound event and experience in itself to lead, remind and reconnect the subject to the eventual goal.

9

9: Ablution pond reflecting the gateway and crown of Jami Mosque, Ahmedabad, once again reminding and reinforcing belief in the eventual goal.

Narratives through notions
Semiotics

In a country enriched by tradition and folklore, almost every aspect of Indian life has a special significance, which is translated into symbolic expressions. Semiotics is, thus, yet another means of communication that, given the plethora of associated values, conjures notions. Metaphors, signs and symbols are visual clues creating allegories, allusions and associations. These create notional realities absolving and overwhelming the obligation of the physical construct–the material reality. Mind wins over matter. For example, an abandoned wall or a tree trunk ceases to be perceived only as a three-dimensional object but assumes new meaning as a holy shrine owing to conjured associations. No longer identified as a tree or a wall, it gets primarily defined as a shrine through overlaid symbols and their implicit communication. The associations and values thus evoked by them convert the hitherto mundane objects to meaningful icons.

1: The sprouting branch of the *tulsi* (basil) and the swastik motif render the wall as a shrine.

2: A banyan tree is considered sacred and revered as a holy place due to its location near a shrine and the association to its implanter.

3: The hollow of a tree trunk is transformed into a shrine with religious motifs, the ritually lit *diya*, lamp, within the multi-point arched doorway.

4: Sanctity of the idols reverberates in the reverence of the tree.

1

2

3

4

5

6

7a

▼7b

Symbols become an added overlay to the spatial construct, further reinforcing communication. For example, at the Queen's Stepwell at Patan, the sequential frames at every floor along the path to the water portray the image of Lord Vishnu under the hood of Sheshnaga–the serpent God–as a consistent visual focus and a reminder of the journey to the *patal lok*–the nether world.

Narratives vitalise actions into experiences. This is illustrated in the ritual of *naman*–the act of paying obeisance through touch–where the involved sense of touch, becomes an additional tool for animating the event. In the Shiv-linga, the *linga* is reflected in the still waters of the *yoni*. During *naman*, the water is touched, creating ripples and thereby unsettling the still *linga* reflection, bringing it to life. Thus, narratives make communication mutually interactive, aptly comprehensible and effervescently vital.

5: A relief on the shaft of the Queen's Stepwell at Patan, depicting Lord Vishnu under Sheshnaga, the king of serpents, framed by the trabeated structure.

6: Ritualistic obeisance to Lord Shiva through the Shiv-linga.

7a & 7b: Symbolism adds a separate layer and, thus, a new dimension to the otherwise flat and uninspiring builtform, transgressing its physicality. Seen here (7a) is the bland adobe and plastered wall of the *bhunga* under construction. This gets transformed into a home through associations, bringing in a sense of place and belonging as seen here on the left.

Dictums
Organizational Principles for Spatial Narratives in Indian Architecture

There are innumerable nuances of builtform through which traditional Indian architecture manifests moods, communicates messages. Narratives built within the space resolutions in traditional architecture can be distilled as generic principles.

Disparate visual and physical axis: The non-linear organization of spaces through the shifting axes of the movement path help gradually unfold vistas. As the visual axis differs from the physical one, locomotion is induced. The interplay of the two achieves simultaneous processes of revelation and concealment, perceived while the person moves through the space. It provides further clues, reinforcing the pursuit of the goal.

Layering for the sequential unfolding of spaces: When the configuration has inbuilt overlays, then in the process of moving through the ensemble, the visitor experiences the unfolding of layers of spaces, which create hierarchies and establish priorities. Baffles, voids and thresholds achieve this by inducing an interactive communication process of encoding and decoding messages between the perceiver and the subject. Each barrier makes one pause, reorient and discover the new facets that keep unfolding through the journey, engaging the visitor in the entire process. The communication is mutual between the onlooker and his environment while the perception is sensorial.

1: Landscape and water elements used effectively as baffles at Bibi-ka-Maqbara, Aurangabad.

2: Ground plane articulation occupying the axial path makes physical movement indirect at Humayun's Tomb in Delhi.

3: Perforated screens, *jalis*, arresting movement while maintaining visual links at Fatehpur Sikri.

4: Non-axial alignments of steps with platforms create circuitous movement and pause points at the Sun Temple, Modhera.

5: Pavilion structure at Kanchipuram placed on the temple axis restricts direct movement.

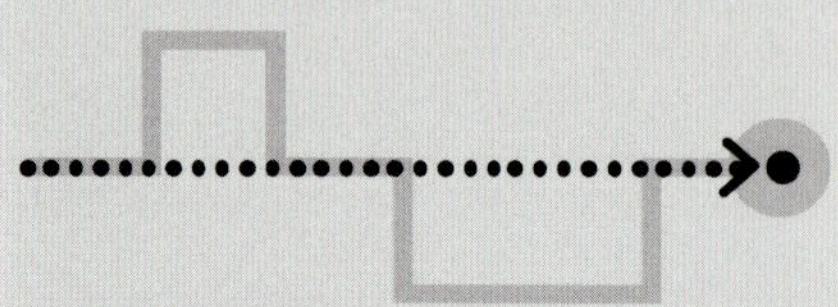

Illustrations a, b, c, and d demonstrate how the destination, though aligned axially from entry, only remains a visual reference on that axis while the physical movement path is shifted from this axis.

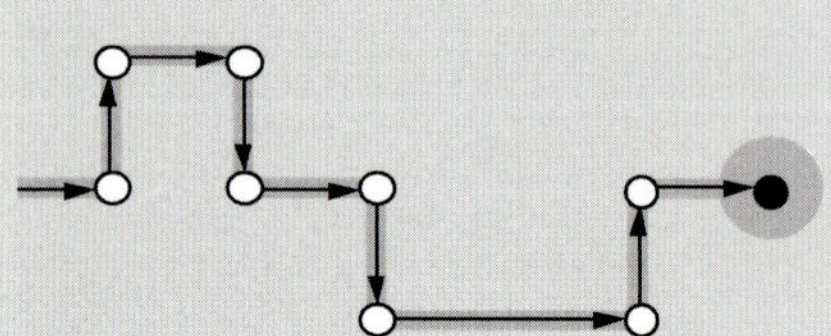

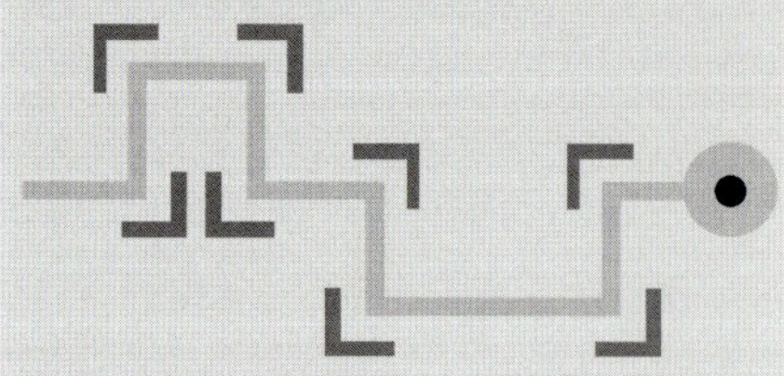

Physical barriers deviate the visual axis through the movement path though the visual continuity is mantained.

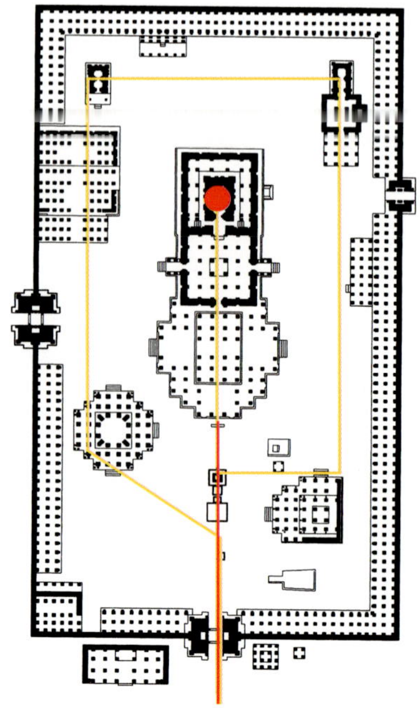

a: Vithalaswami Temple, Hampi

1

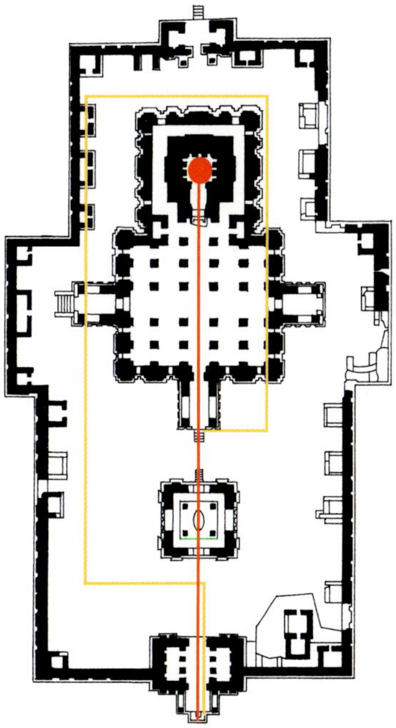

b: Virupaksha Temple, Pattadakal

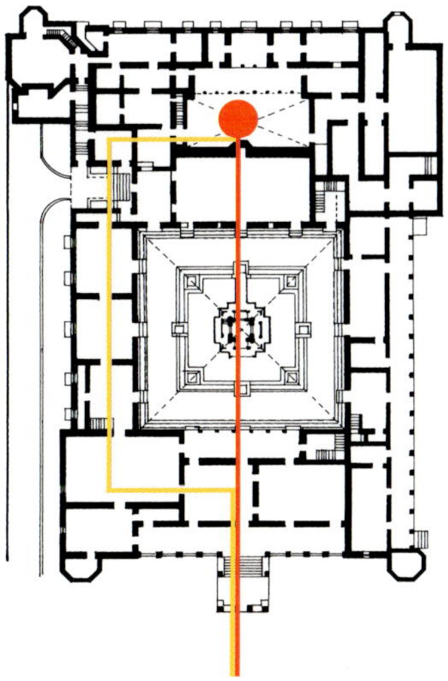

c: Udai Bilas Palace, Dungarpur

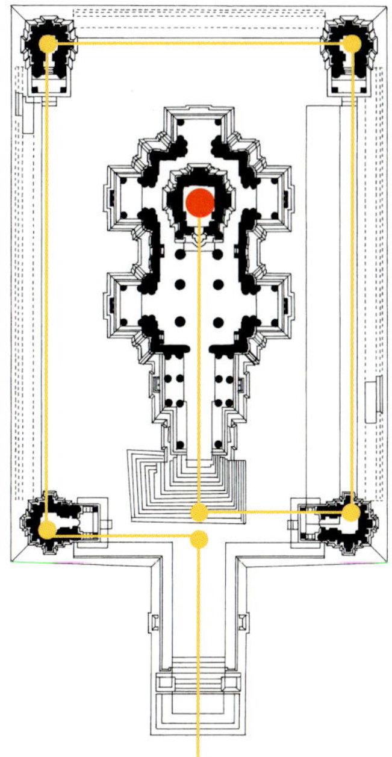

d: Lakshmana Temple, Khajuraho

2

3

4

5

MOVEMENT–A KEY TO CONDITIONING OF THE MIND: While the indirect path of movement creates a sense of discovery, the increased length of the path also helps in conditioning of the mind. In Indian architecture, movement holds the key. It allows for time to overlay space. The dynamics of time over space renders the space ever-changing and fresh. The changed mood of the same space over time also makes it flexible for varied use, hence allowing for effective optimization of space resource such as through multiple usage of the same space through time. The journey, to a certain degree defined through the space with pauses, turns and shifts, becomes a ritual in itself and engages the individual perceiver through these processes.

CHOICES OF MOVEMENT PATH FOR PERSONAL AND INTUITIVE EXPERIENCE: Thresholds reorient and help one reaffirm one's bearings. They provide clues and informed choices for individual preferences and personal pursuits. These allow the comprehension of space with personal references, its experience at one's own pace and its interpretation as an individual pursuit. This makes the entire communication process personal and thereby intuitively experiential–a welcome characteristic of any design in a pluralistic society to confirm/adapt to multiple value systems.

KINESTHETICS AS THE ORGANIZATIONAL AND PROPORTIONING TOOL: The movement path invokes a dynamic perception of space. This aspect of kinesthetics provides for varied compositions and constantly-changing points of visual references. The perspectival effects in the visual frames and their strategic alignment often provide a basis for the proportioning of spaces and locating pause points where special compositional or visual effects are pronounced. This marks a characteristic departure from the geometric plan resolution to a three-dimensional visual coordination. The latter approach comes closest to actual perception at eye level and thereby influences the desired conditioning of mind and behaviour.

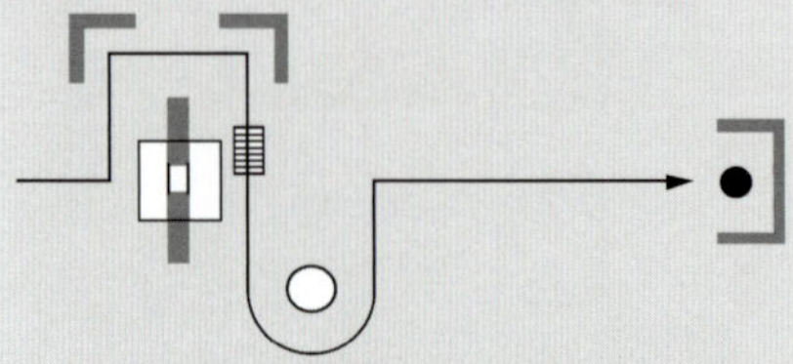

The winding movement through a series of spaces creates varied mental conditioning as in the temple sequences.

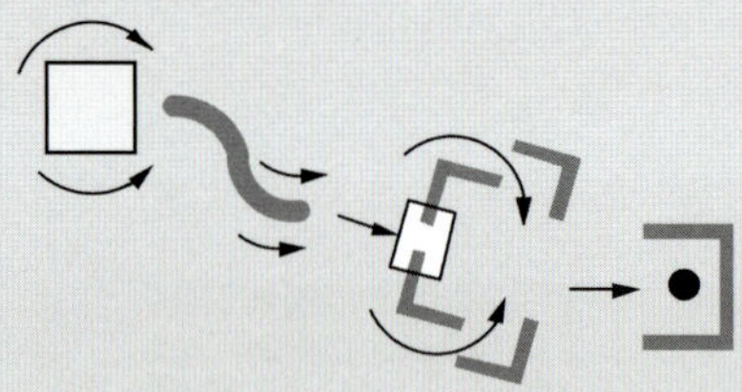

Choices of movement path allow the individual freedom of relating in one's own way.

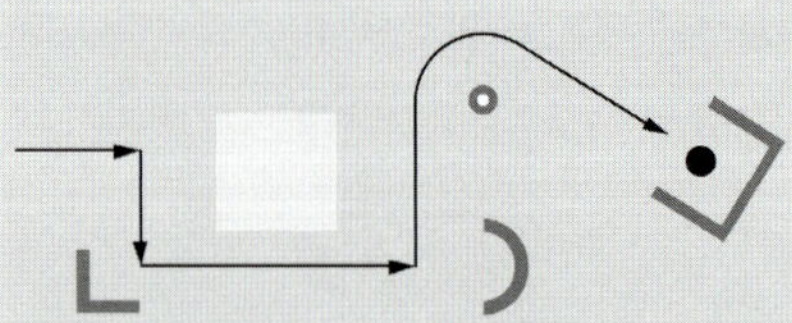

Movement as a critical feature to induce kinetic perception of space.

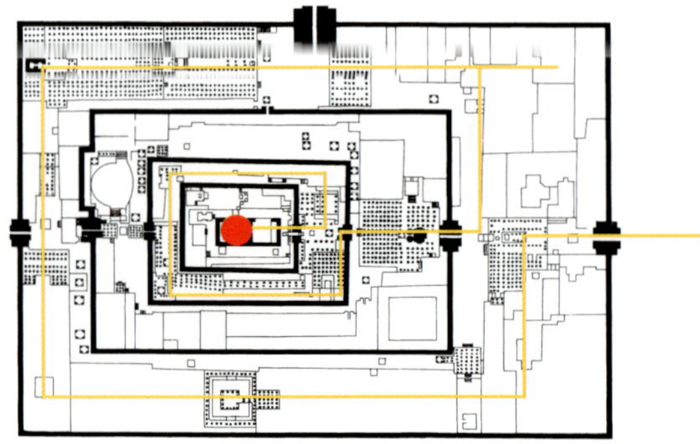

Ranganatha Temple, Srirangam

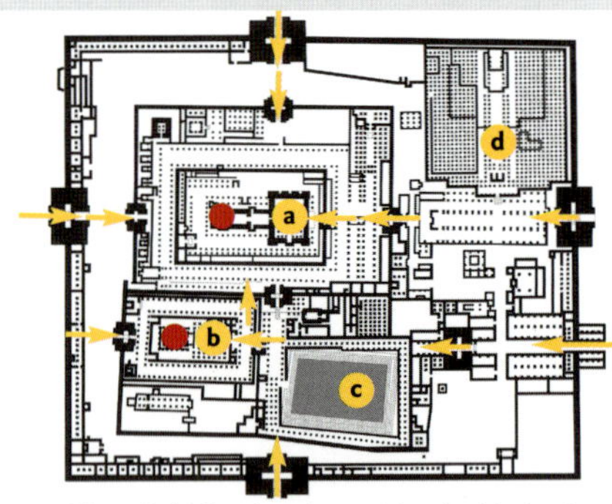

Meenakshi Sundareshwara Temple, Madurai
a: Sundareshwara shrine **b**: Meenakshi shrine
c: Tank **d**: Thousand-pillared hall

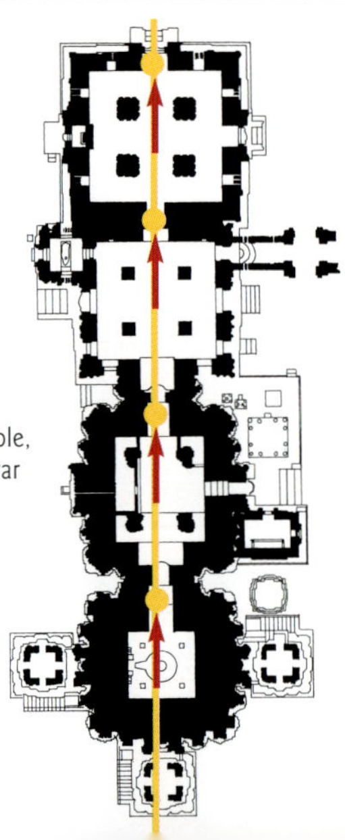

Lingaraja Temple, Bhubhaneshwar

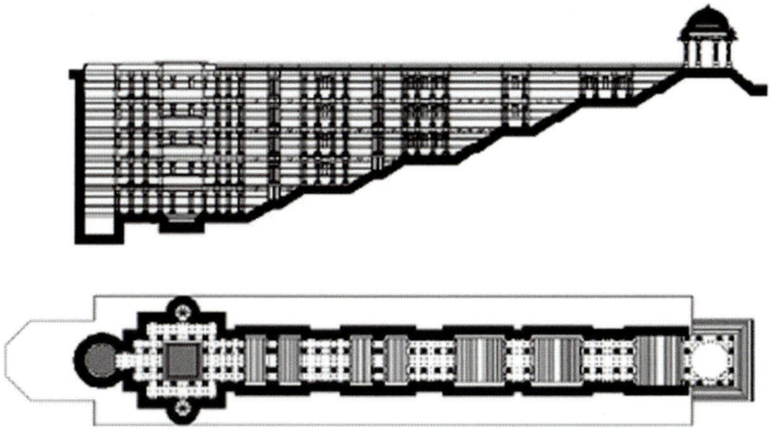

Dada Harir Stepwell , Ahmedabad

1: Water channel along the movement path reflects the crown of the Taj Mahal as a visual reminder of the destination.

2: Minaret of the Taj Mahal is revealed and visually framed at the landing of the entrance stairway.

3: Framed view of the terrace pavilion at the stair landing of Jahaz Mahal, Mandu.

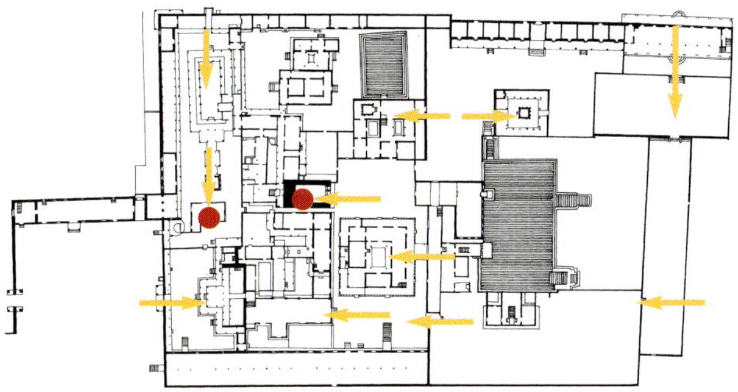

Padmanabhapuram Palace, Thiruvananthapuram

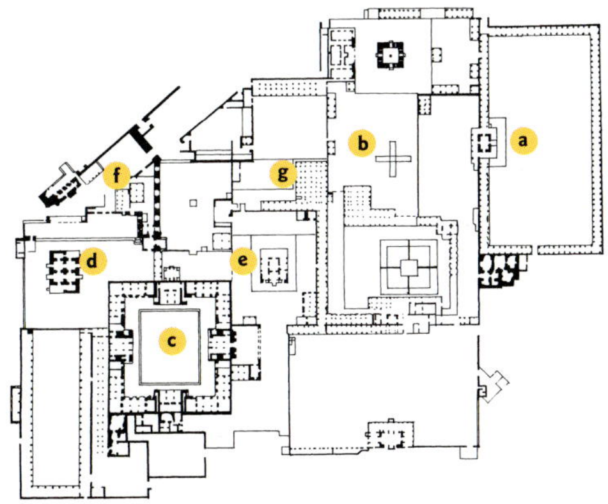

Royal complex, Fatehpur Sikri, where multi-axial plan organization provides various thresholds, helping in reorienting the bearing and creating new preferences and pauses. **a**: Diwan-i-am, **b**: Daulat Khana and Diwan-i-khas, **c**: Jodhabai's Palace, **d**: House of Birbal, **e**: House of Miryam, **f**: Nagina Masjid, **g**: Panch Mahal

1

2

3

Composite schema of centre and sub-centres through layering as well as links

Indoors integrated with outdoors through landscaping and light:

Integration of indoors with outdoors and the unbuilt with the built space provide for mutual counterpoints. Unbuilt space, such as courtyards function independently within themselves as individual foci and yet interconnected systems of courtyards create a larger space structure, as an integral part of the overall space organization. The outdoors, through landscape elements, vegetation and the play of light remains a dynamic phenomenon due to seasonal variations, climatic conditions, the varying position of the sun and the altering intensity of light. These render the static built space different and changed at all times.

Semiotics as an associational overlay:

Sensorial stimuli, operating at a physical and human plane, remain perceptible universally. However, inlaid messages in the form of motifs and symbols do not share the same fate. Symbols operate within the realm of familiarity and association, often involving socio-cultural conditioning. Symbols and metaphors overlaid as an extra layer on the spatially narrative builtform create an associational bond and reinforce the conceptual underpinning of the experiential. They add a patina of meaning charging the mental faculties and deepening the understanding of the context, thus making the experience holistic, that is, sensorial as well as spiritual. The aspects of time over space overlaid by symbolic overtones, lend varied associational meaning to the same space configuration through such conditioning.

1: The Om symbol atop an outcrop of boulders grants it a shrine status.

2: Sculptures flanking the corridor at the Madurai temple create a celestial ambience as one walks through.

3: Spiritual aspects interwoven into daily life using traditional motifs in the vernacular dwellings of Kutchchh.

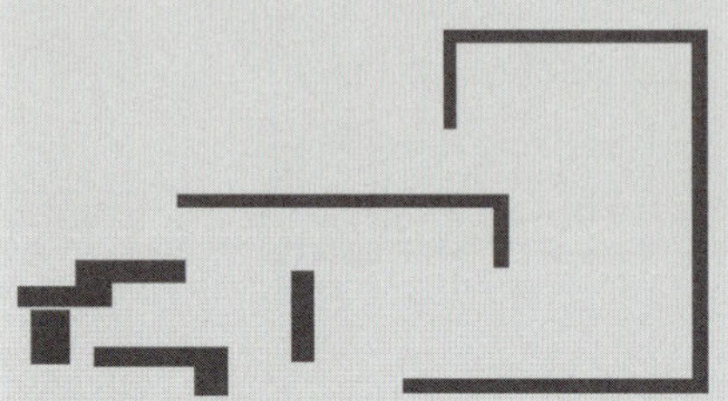

Indoors integrated with outdoors through landscaping and light.

The swastika, a Hindu holy symbol, has different connotations as soon as turned at 45 degrees due to its associational value to the Nazi movement.

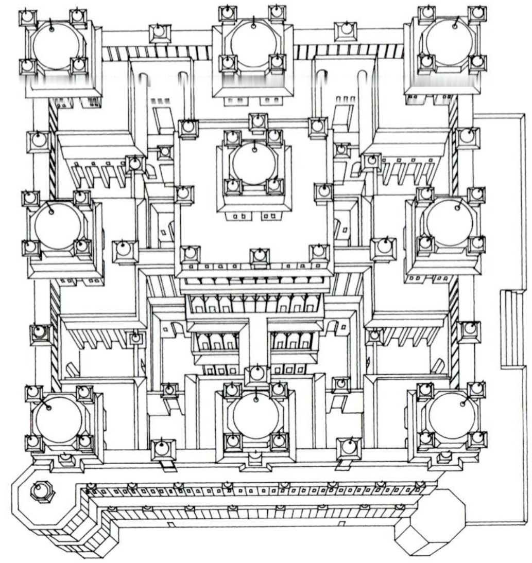

The Govind Mandir, Datia, where the external world is recreated within through a composition of the built and the unbuilt.

1

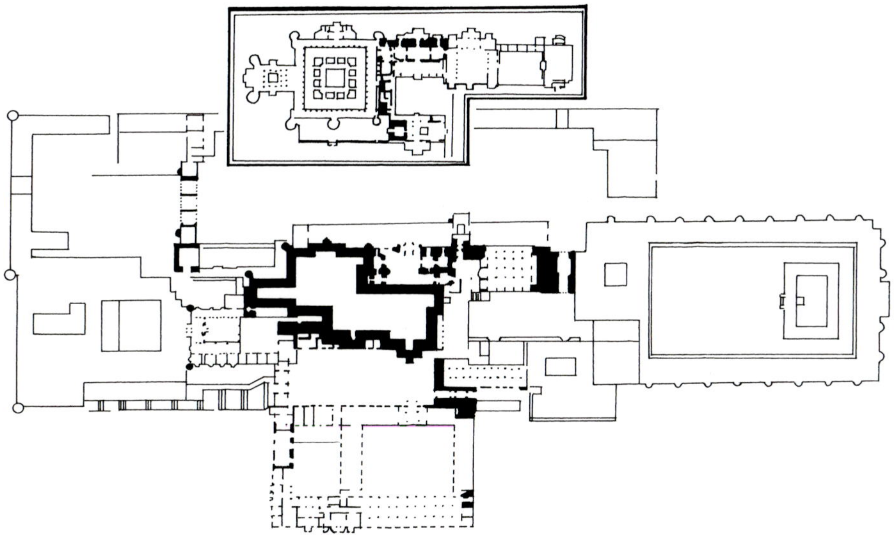

Series of courts and built spaces effectively evoke different moods at the City Palace,Udaipur.

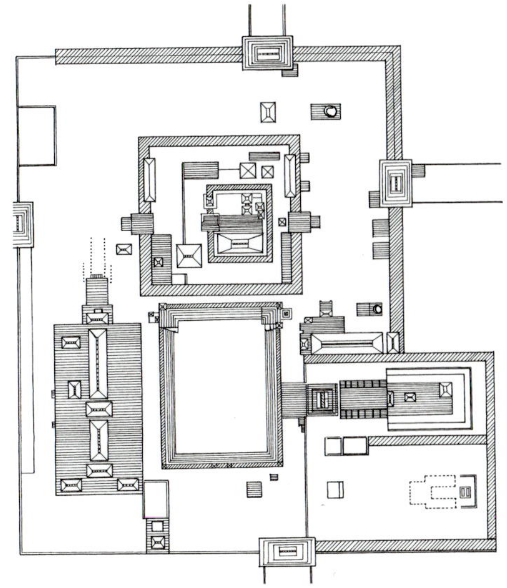

Spirituality involving its devotee through the use of contained courts and temple spaces at the Nataraja Temple, Chidambaram.

2

3

Application

The following is an enquiry into the spatial narratives–sensorial, experiential and associational perceptions and the processes of encoding-decoding messages–that characterise traditional Indian architecture and render it timeless. The examples represent early and evolved architectural ensembles from religious, royal and utilitarian structures.

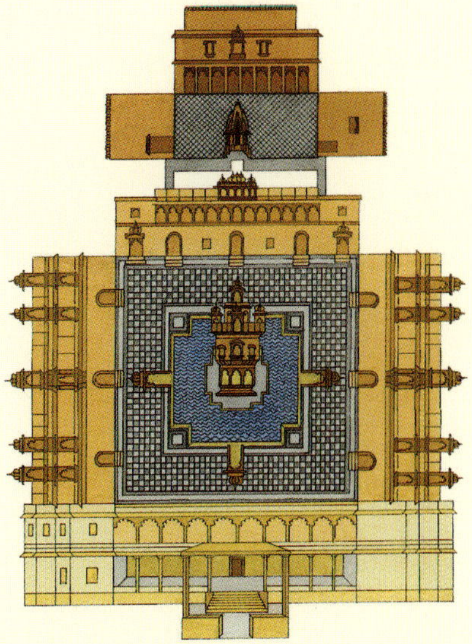

RUDABAI STEPWELL
A D A L A J

◄ Vignettes as framed by spatial elements at the Adalaj Stepwell.

► A miniature style impression narrating the spatial sequences.

The Context

The stepwell–a well accessible through steps–is a building typology which is most commonly found in the western hot, arid parts of India. Essentially a device to contain water, it is exalted to become a socio-religious institution–owing largely to its architectural manifestations. One such stepwell is located at Adalaj. Formerly on a caravan route from Ahmedabad to Patan, the then capital of Gujarat, it was built in 1499 by Rudabai, the wife of a Hindu Rajput king, Vikramsinh Vaghela. The prevailing Islamic rule created an interesting fusion of Hindu and Islamic architectural styles peculiar to the Sultanate regime in Gujarat which came to be identified as Indo-Saracenic architecture. Hindu craftsmanship and trabeated construct-ion techniques were combined with geometric principles and floral patterns from Islam. As subterranean architecture, it provides effective natural insulation through earth mass in the hot, dry climate. The five-storeyed structure is braced with cross beams all along its length to retain the earth. These structural ties double up as resting platforms for travellers. For women fetching water they become interactive places for socializing, offering a chance to chat and relieve their stresses. This transformed a mundane routine into an enjoyable event. With associations to water, *patal lok*–the nether world and the womb of Mother Earth–the journey conjures the sense of ablution and the well assumes the status of a shrine. Thus a simple utilitarian device is elevated to the status of a social as well as a religious node.

1: Niches with deities and *jharokha*-like spaces evoke interactive social and religious conjunctions.

2: Isometric view of the Adalaj Stepwell showing the massing and relative assembly of its architectural components.

1

2 ►

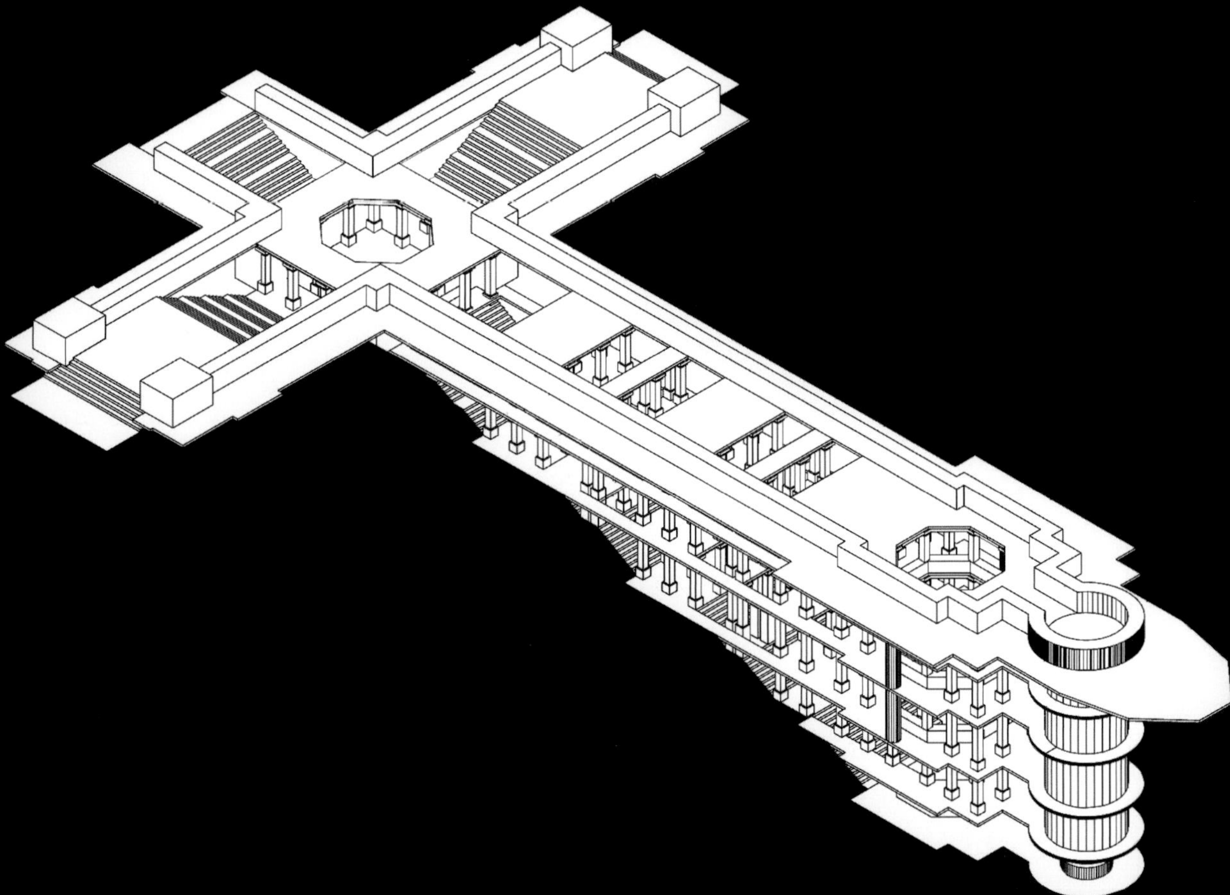

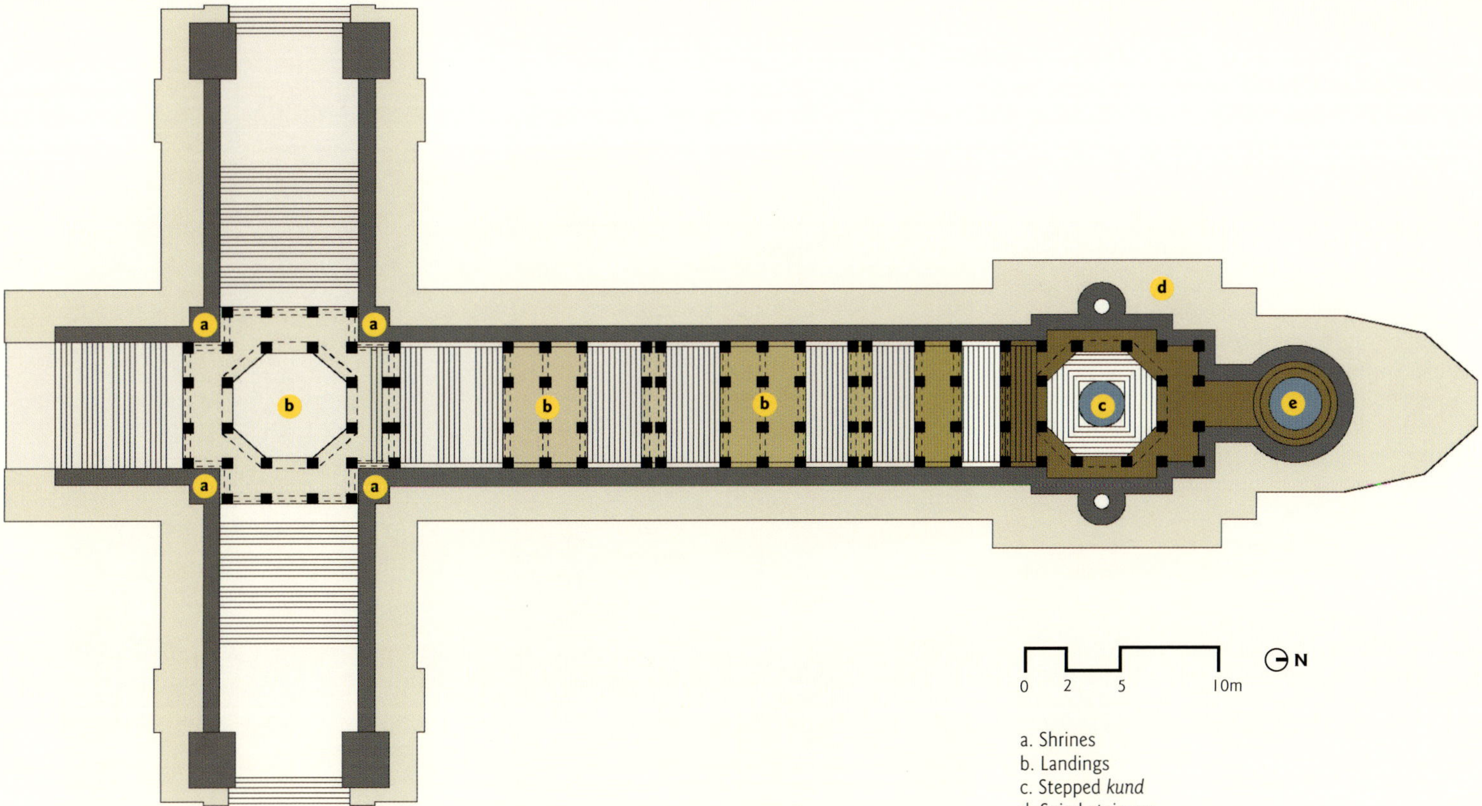

Plan

Facing page: The highly ornate octagonal shaft over the water source is overlooked by balconies on each floor.

Section

The stepwell at Adalaj is a five-storeyed ensemble beneath the earth. Built in stone through the trabeated technique of construction, it uses stone columns and beams essentially to counter the compressive stresses of the earth. Availability and manoeuverability of the rectilinear stone beams determined the spans and thereby necessitated the introduction of intermediate rows of column support. This creates a spatial rhythm along the length. Similarly, the lateral braces and wide platforms become the struts to shore the retaining walls resisting the lateral thrust of the earth. This breaks down the enclosed volume into a number of subspaces as well as sets up successive visual frames.

1: A sandstone, trabeated construction creating visual portals through column and beam assembly.

2: The cross platforms and beams act as structure to shore the embankment walls against the thrust of the earth.

3: An exploded isometric view of the stepwell showing the individual components which form the composite. From bottom: the well shafts, the sloping stair-mass, the various layers of colonnaded structure with intermediate platforms relative to the ground plane.

◄1 2▲ 3►

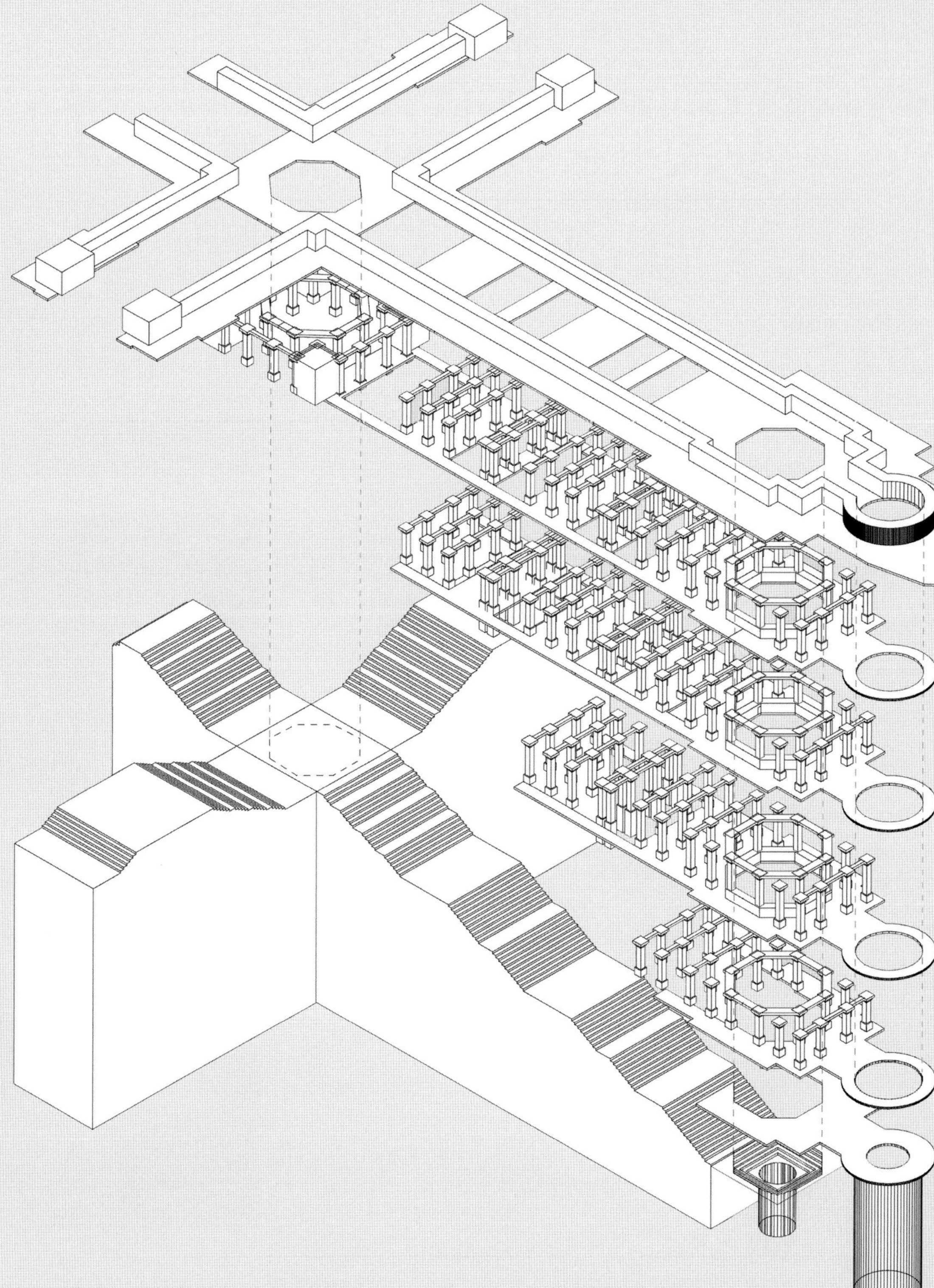

Kinesthetics

Spatially, the stepwell remains one of the most profound architectural statements. Despite its functional obsolescence of fetching water in today's context, it continues to inspire visitors after more than five centuries. Transcending time and space, it has rendered itself timeless, essentially through its spatial attributes and the experience of moving through the same. These experiences are shared trans-culturally by all, at a basic human plane, without any familiarity with the context or any knowledge of the history. This also makes it universal, where communication between the subject and the perceiver is inherently decipherable. It is the journey, the process of moving through the space, which in itself becomes the event.

The clues for movement, inherent in the space, are revealed sequentially. This gradual unfolding of spaces creates a sense of curiosity within the perceivers and involves them in the process. A dialogue is established between the subject and the perceiver through the mutual process of encoding and decoding of messages, thus making the entire process interactive as well as the discovery very personal and intuitive.

At the Adalaj Stepwell, the only visible clue above the ground is the pair of large pilasters flanking a wide flight of steps. They become the inviting portal to climb the steps leading to a platform. The plinth platform then leads the descent through the steps and retaining sidewalls. The first flight of steps descends to a square platform with columns supporting an octagonal frame, which would once have been the base for a dome. This becomes the first point of pause. Surrounded on three sides by the inclined planes of rising steps the node leaves only one side open to approach. This is perpendicular to the axis of previous movement and thus involves a shift in the visual as well as the movement path. It is at this place that the space starts its dynamic illusory interplay between the visual axis and the movement path. The new axis is marked by a series of descending steps and intermittent platforms located along the horizontal visual axis.

Although there is a straight linear symmetrical organization of elements along the horizontal axis, the visual references continuously change due to inclined movement (through simultaneous displacement of the horizontal and vertical axis) at every step. While the sight lines extend through the entire length of the well, the visual frame constantly changes with the changing eye levels, perspectival alignments and the resultant visual composition all along its depth.

1: The two pilasters flanking the wide flight of steps is the first external clue denoting the entry.

2: A downward movement is revealed only upon climbing these initial steps.

3: The pavilion-like structure with square platform and octagonal beam frame punctuates the node as the confluence of three movement paths.

4: The fenestrated lateral ties create continuous horizontal frames giving delusions about the actual height.

5: The visual composition changes with respect to depth of vision, aided by differing intensities of light with progressive descent.

6: Revelation of the water at the end where the connection of the earth to the sky is made through light and reflection (view from top towards bottom.)

1

2

3

4

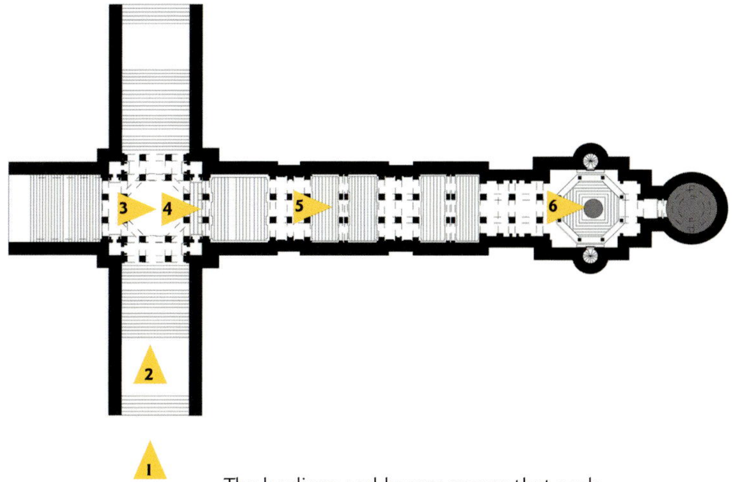

5

6 ►

The landings and beams ensure that each flight of steps reveal only themselves and the immediate landing while the subsequent flights of steps and water remain concealed from the cone of vision. Portals created by the trabeated column and beam construction to shore the sidewalls retaining the earth exalt to become key spatial elements. The stone columns and beams provide the visual frames, which enhance the sense of depth by providing intermediate visual references.

With such changing visual frames the descent of five floors brings one *en-face* the actual water source. As a termination of the journey, steps flank the water on all four sides making the well the notional centre and the focus, with the shaft connecting vertically up to the sky and down into the water.

Following pages:

Left: The well shaft with pulleys to fetch water for cattle and farming.

Right: Compositions as framed at key nodes such as arrival node (a), intermediate platform (b), descending flights of steps (c, d, e, f) and the water *kund* (g).

a

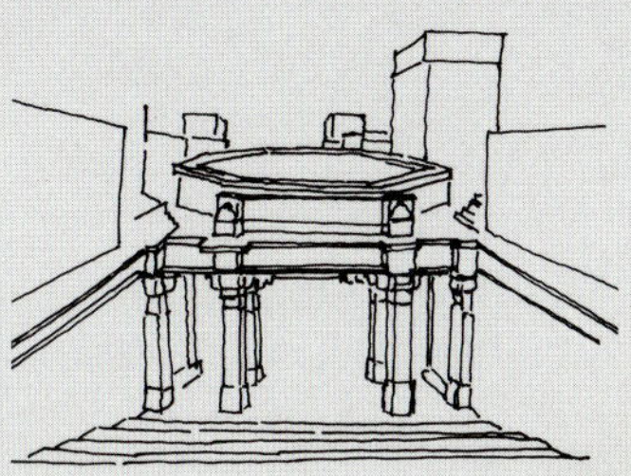

b

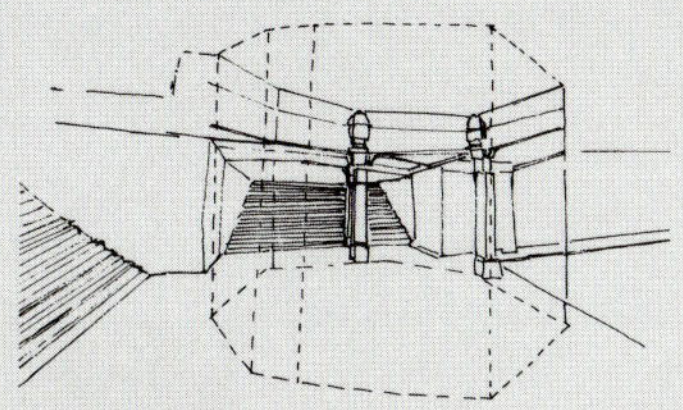

c

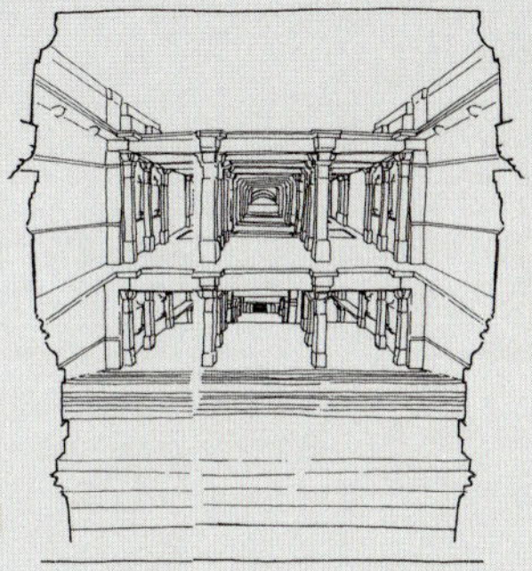

d

e

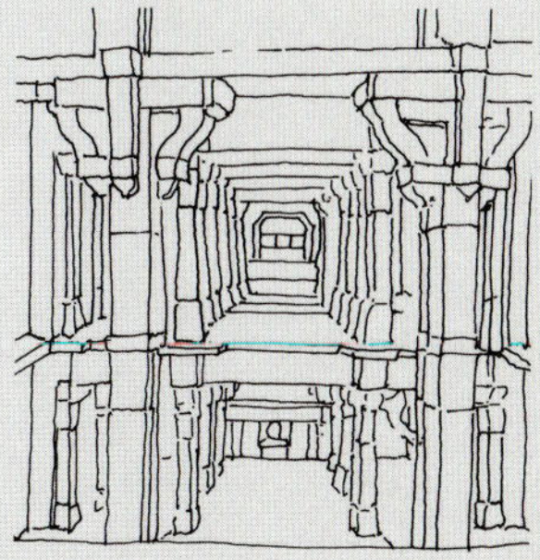

f

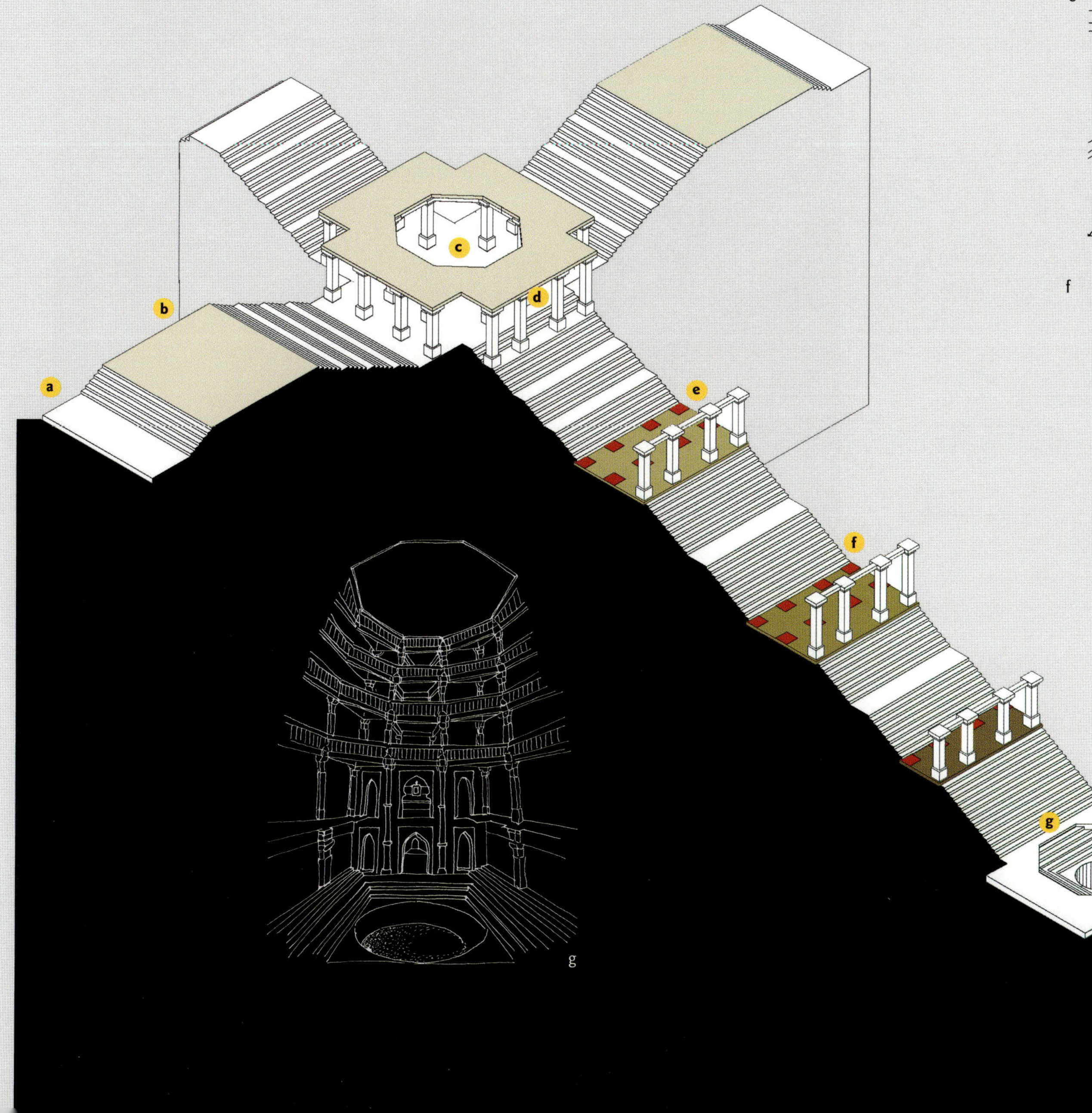

The shoring walls along with the platforms and trabeation provide the sense of enclosure to a space essentially open to sky. The perception of enclosure is further reinforced by the decreasing intensity of light as one descends towards the water. The harshness of light subdues as one progresses further and deeper into the space, making the path progressively vertical, more intimate and contained.

The stepwell's timelessness is attributed to the freshness offered by the variations of visual frames as well as the integration of the relationship between light and the unbuilt spaces, where the sun is the consistent variable as it changes position and intensity from morning to evening and from summer to winter. During mid-day the vertical rays of the sun penetrate deeper into the shaft, while in the mornings and evenings the light moves towards the edges. This makes the otherwise static symmetric composition perceptibly dynamic with varying outdoor conditions.

The variation of visual frames accentuates the varying effects of the sun's light over time and season. It is to this dynamic that we can attribute the stepwell's universality.

1: Gradations of light from top to bottom as seen in the octagonal well shaft.

2: Sectional isometric indicating changing intensities of light along with increasing enclosure.

1

2 ►

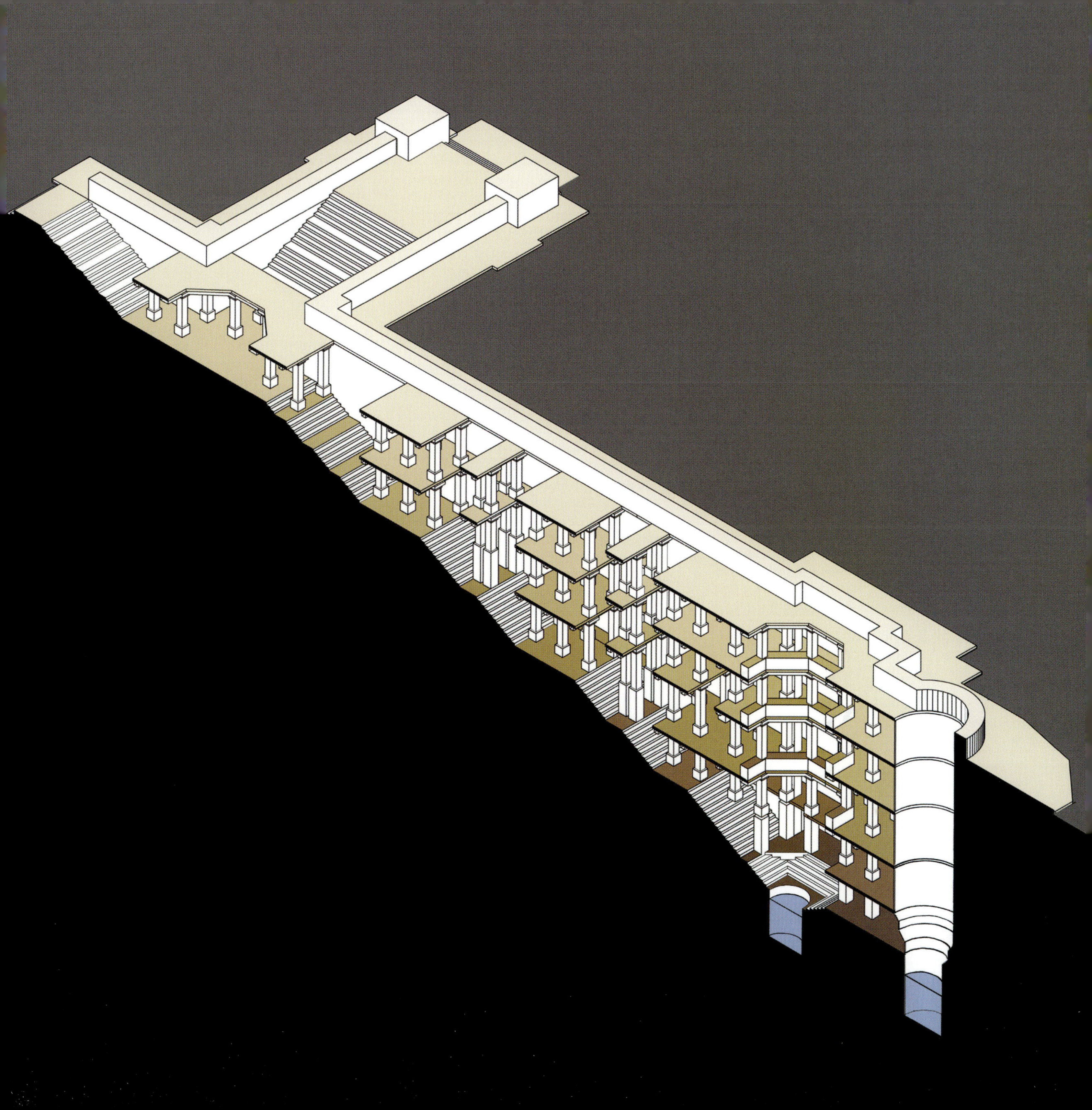

Notions

The journey of descent conditions the mind to an increasing sense of penetration into the ground. These increasing sensations of enclosure, descent, intimacy and dimness contrast with the extroverted nature of the flat ground outside. The experience of introspection is further enhanced by the visual information on the layers of entablature, replete with carvings and symbols. To a Hindu, stepwells have two associations. One of ablution–purgative cleansing in holy water–and the association to *patal lok*, or the nether world. These associations are conjured by the water-related motifs recurring in the carved relief. For example, at Adalaj, the statuette of Lord Ganesha marks the beginning of the journey, and is located at the top rim level of the well, in direct line of sight at the beginning of the descent, while the shoring wall edges have plaques depicting water urns. The frieze panel over the beam depicts churning (symbolizing Samudra-Manthana, churning of the ocean). The base of the well, at the water level, is carved with motifs of fish.

These symbols and details function as constant reminders of one's presence within the realm of water and create the mood, ambience and the mental frame so that finally reaching the water is symbolically an ablution in itself–a holy dip into the water. Water, reflecting the sky, and filtered sunlight exhibit the bi-unity of extremes, water and fire as opposites notionally co-exist as counter references.

In the dry, arid lands of Gujarat, water is a life-giving resource–the epitome of the Creative Force. This is expressed in the other association of the stepwell–that of fertility–the womb of Mother Earth. These notions are conjured through plaques depicting goddesses and symbols of femininity. These are still worshipped and their blessings sought by newlyweds during nuptial ceremonies. Thus, through these notions and conditioning of the mind, the well as a utilitarian object gets elevated to a shrine. Nourishing physically as well as spiritually, it communicates beyond its functional and structural dictates. The sum total of the experience is sensorial as well as spiritual, invigorating the senses as well as the being. The meaning is in the journey itself and not necessarily the destination. The destination is not an end in itself, it is rather an excuse.

1

2

3

4

5

6

7

1: Ganesha, the remover of obstacles, is appeased at the initiation of any venture. Here, he is placed directly along the visual axis at the beginning of the descent.

2 and 3: Shakti, the divine mother and creative energy behind all life forms, is revered at the shrine, on the flanking walls.

4: Nine *kumbha* (pots), symbolizing the nine forms of Shakti, also reinforce associations of the water-world.

5: Manthana–the churning sequence as a reminder of the water-world.

6: Fish symbolizing and heralding the arrival at the water-world.

7: The symbolic unification of sky and water at the base through reflection.

8: Spatial sequences depicted in a miniature style impression.

9: Symbols and their respective placement at the Adalaj Stepwell.

Pages 54-55: The return journey marked by the ascent of flights is an experience from dark to bright, from the enclosed to the open.
Photo courtesy: Raajesh Moothan

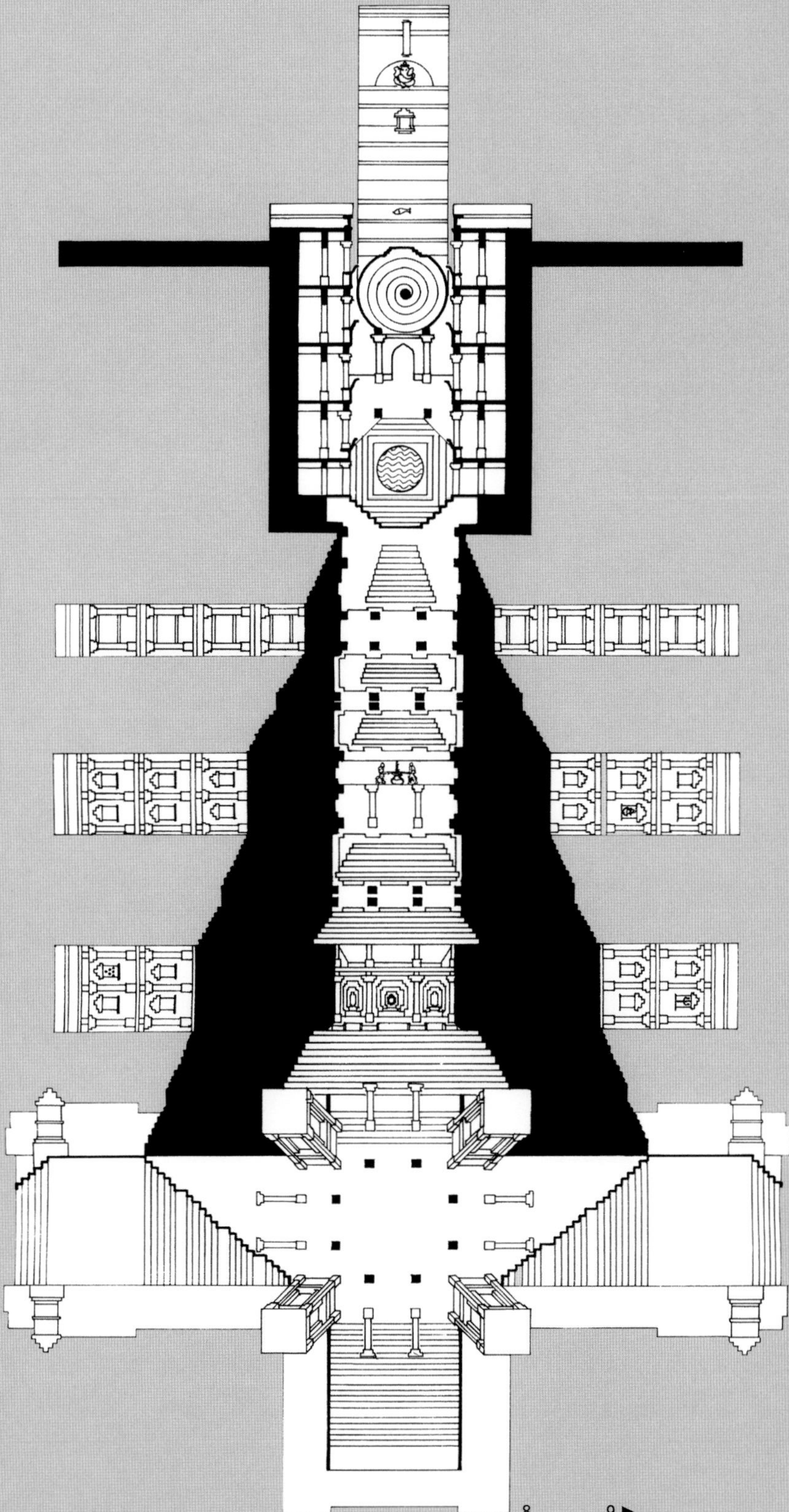

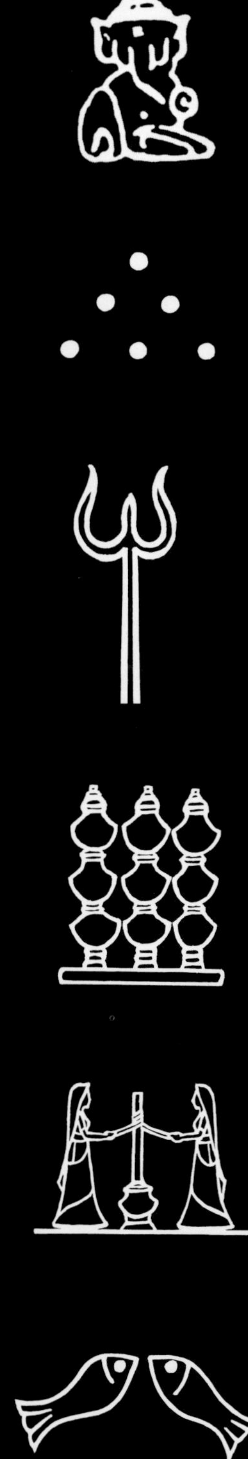

KAILASH TEMPLE
ELLORA

◄ The poetry of contrasts. Finely carved out form contrasts sharply against the rough-hewn rock.

► Artist's impression in the miniature style, showing masses and voids at Kailash Temple, Ellora.

THE CONTEXT

The Kailash Temple at Ellora–an entire precinct consisting of both free-standing and hollowed out forms carved out of the living rock of an entire hillside–is the epitome of rock-cut architecture in India and the most aggrandized manifestation of the technique. A phantasmagoric composition of mysterious spaces, sculpted surfaces and mythical monsters, the temple is a treasure-house of visual treats and spatial experiences, apart from ritual overlays and symbolic significance. Built in the reign of Dantidurga and Krishna I, between A.D. 757 and 773 and dedicated to Lord Shiva, the main deity of the precinct, it draws freely from references of the Virupaksha Temple at Hampi and other Pallava temples. Unlike the smaller varieties of the built-up architecture of the period, this magnificent example of the Dravidian style of architecture is the largest monolithic temple in India. The complex consists of a large scooped-out enclosure measuring about 100 metres by 75 metres cut into the rocky slopes, leaving the free-standing masses consisting of the Nandi shrine and the main temple. The narrow trench of open space running round it forms a circumambulatory path at ground level. There are sub-spaces carved out on the north and south rock-faces. These shrines and relief iconography depict secondary deities and Lord Shiva and his anthropomorphic forms and bring to life scenes from his vast and complex mythology. A colonnaded corridor is cut into the periphery of the rock-face at the rear of the scooped-out enclosure at ground level, running along the three sides of the base of the temple. The entire temple is oriented east-west. The temple complex is enclosed on three sides by the rock mass and a wall-like barrier on the fourth. Access into the precinct is gained through a small opening doorway in this otherwise totally blank and unwelcoming wall, a penetrable mass defining the extent of the complex. Free-standing forms of elephants and decorative obelisks flanking the Nandi shrine exhibit an innovative adaptation of the construction technique and a variation over the temple typology of the period. It also forms an integral feature unique to the ensemble. The entrance gateway forms a bridge at the upper level to connect to the rock-face on either side.

1 2 ►

1: The Kailash Temple at Ellora is an ensemble of rock-cut, scooped-out and free-standing structures.

2: Lower level plan with cross-section showing the built and unbuilt relationships.

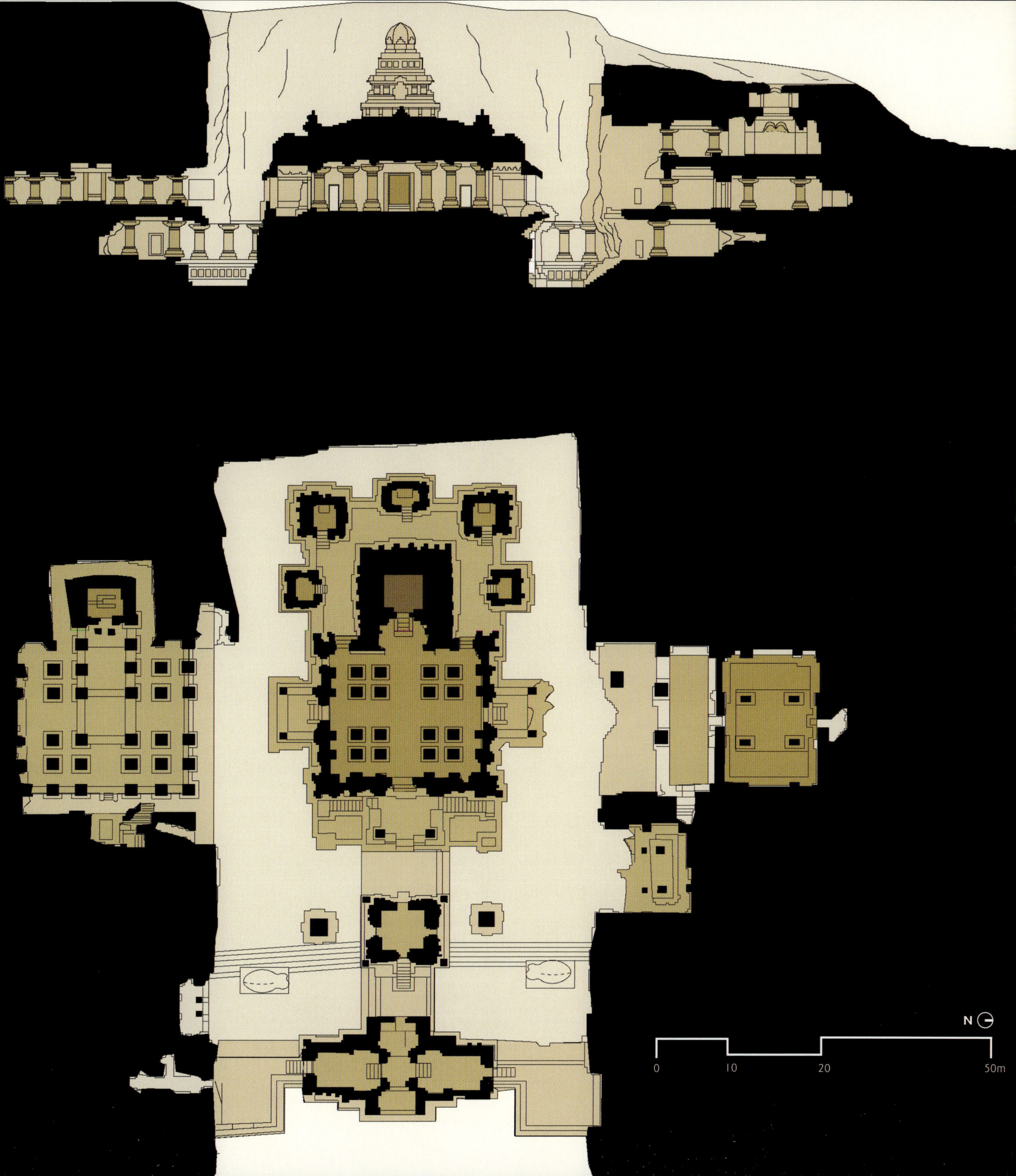
N
0
10
20
50m

The temple precinct, although comprised of many parts, is still perceived as a single complex. This is due to various factors–enclosure of the rock-face, consistency of material, contiguity of surface, etc. The entrance gate, the Nandi shrine, the main temple, the decorated obelisks, the statuesque elephants, the scooped-out shrines and the colonnaded corridors are components of the overall schema. These components by themselves can also be further dissociated into progressively smaller parts and components. But each of these parts behaves as a self-contained whole, be it spatially or elementally, a coherent entity with an independent identity which, in spite of being part of a larger scheme, exhibits a wholesome totality. This manner of space and design articulation is a manifestation of the Hindu notion of concentric existence, of worlds within worlds, the Brahman and the Atman.

UPPER LEVEL PLAN

a: Nandi *mandapa*
b: *Maha mandapa*
c: *Garbhagriha*
d: Sub-shrines
e: Bridge
f: Lankeshwara Cave
g: Shrine for River Goddess
h: *Yagnashala*

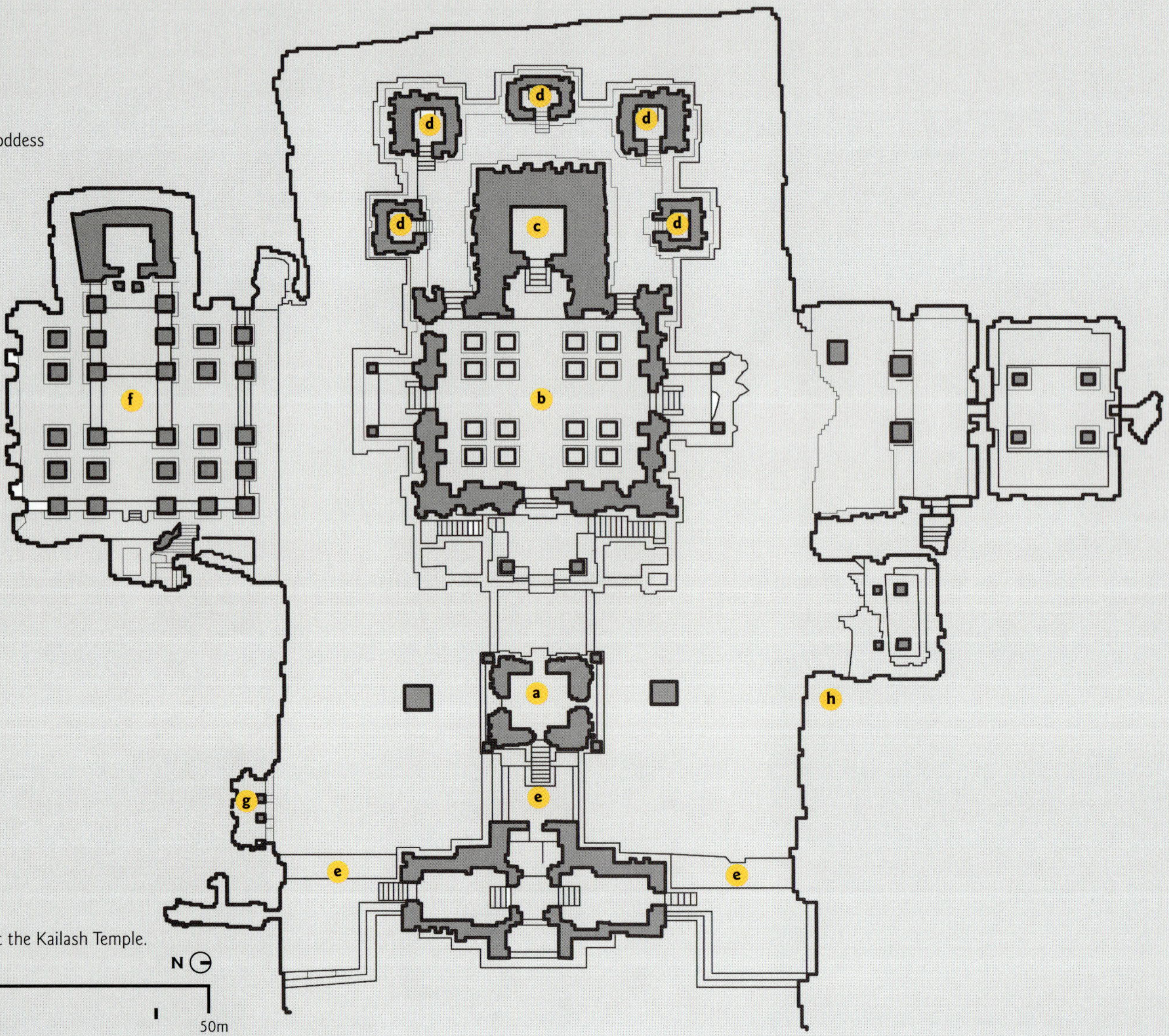

Location of spaces at the Kailash Temple.

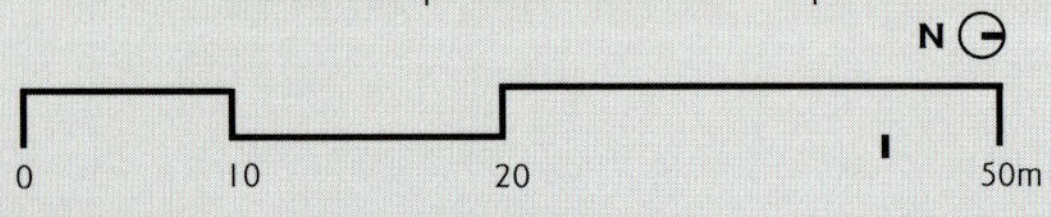

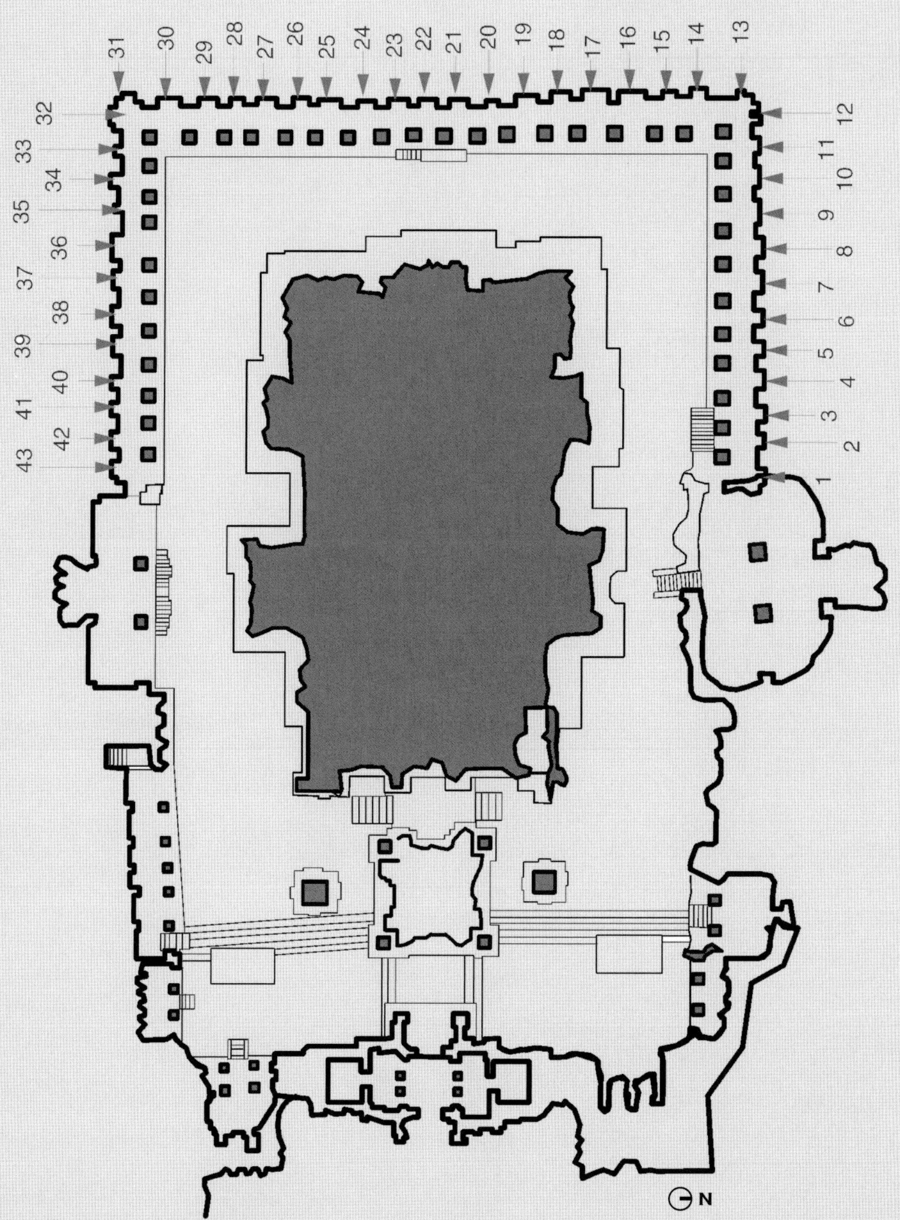

Location of various deities at the Kailash Temple.

Lower level Plan

1. Annapurna
2. Shiva as Balaji
3. Vishnu four-armed
4. Varaha raising Prithvi
5. Vishnu on Garuda
6. Yamuna
7. Four-armed Vishnu
8. Sheshnarayan
9. Narsimha
10. Three-faced Brahma
11. Shiva on Nandi
12. Ardhanarishwara
13. Kal Bhairava
14. Kapal Bhairava
15. Shiva with *trishula*
16. Siddhi yogini Bhairava
17. Batuk Bhairava
18. Bhupal Bhairava
19. Shiva and Parvati
20. Mahadeva four-armed
21. Brahma with *hamsa*
22. Shiva with *naga* and Nandi
23. Shiva
24. Shiva with *trishula*
25. Shiva with snake
26. Shiva with flaming *linga*
27. Shiva holding *damru*, club and bell
28. Shiva and Parvati sitting together
29. Sadashiva
30. Virabhadra
31. Marriage of Shiva and Parvati
32. Shiva defending Markandeya
33. Shiva and Kiratas
34. Shiva and Parvati playing *chausar*
35. Shiva and Parvati sitting together
36. Shiva and Parvati with Ravana shaking Kailash
37. Rishi Muchukund
38. Shiva and Parvati facing each other
39. Shiva with cobra and rosary
40. Shiva and Parvati with Nandi couchant below
41. Shiva and Parvati with *linga*
42. Shiva with Parvati on left knee
43. Kneeling figure of Ravana upholding *salunkha*

The Realms

The configuration scheme of the temple complex can be experienced as a consecutive series of perceivably distinct realms, both spatially and notionally. These realms, though distinct, bleed and blend into each other in a subtle but definite manner, gradually diffusing into one another, with the transition points demarcated as thresholds. The entrance portal, a distinct space in itself, is the primary transition from the outside to the inside. By itself, it is perceived as a space with carved niches and sitting platforms on either side with high plinths. This passage is connected by a threshold to the entrance foyer, a small single height space covered by an overhead bridge, which acts as a verandah or open courtyard to the upper level. This is a point of transition from the profane to the sacred. The entire open-to-sky space is revealed on coming out from below the single height volume at ground level and registers as a complete entity. A datum to bring together the different agglomerates of the precinct, giving access to different parts and at the same time fusing them into a singular whole. The individual scooped-out spaces, with their separate access stairs and platforms, appear disparate, but still conform to the overall scheme in the manner of their opening details, monolithic materialistic consistency, similarity of motifs and elements repeatedly occurring in different parts of the precinct.

The main temple and Nandi shrine, being at a higher level, take the visitor above the ground plane. Accessed by a narrow flight of stairs, it articulates another variation in the understanding of the complex–a transition from the mundane to the celestial, human to the sacred. The physical act of climbing allegorically emphasises the ascent to the heavens. The articulation of spaces at the upper level creates nodes, which demarcate and distinguish the main from the sub-spaces. Diverse techniques of surface treatments such as carvings, relief motifs, iconography and rendering provide adequate visual clues for the visitor to decipher the extent, significance and sanctity of each realm. This entire sequence of subtly-crafted distinctions between notional significance and spatial reality, gradually merging into one other and thus threading together one continuing experience, is another distinct feature of Hindu architecture.

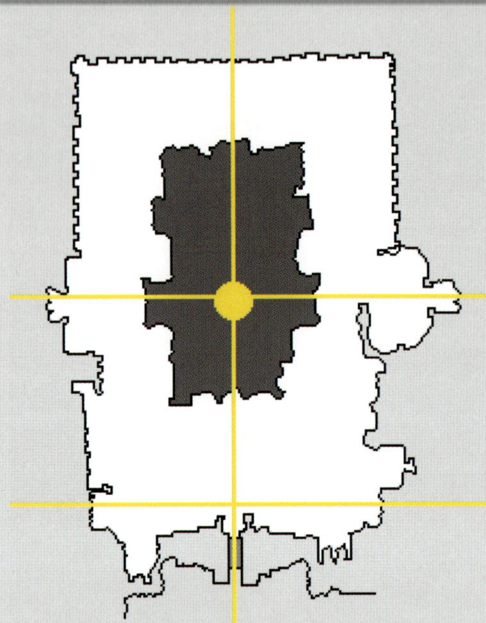
2

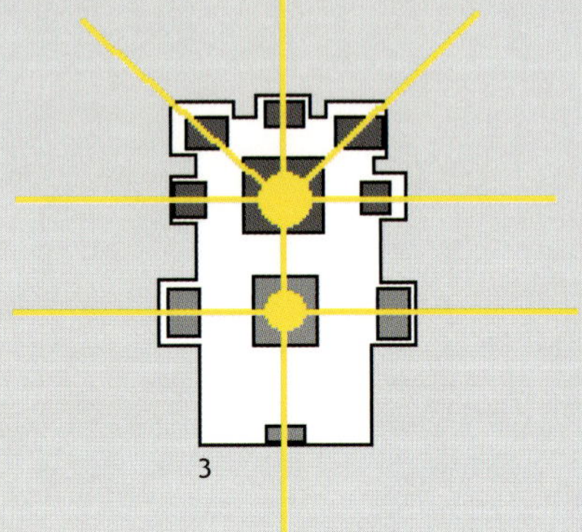
3

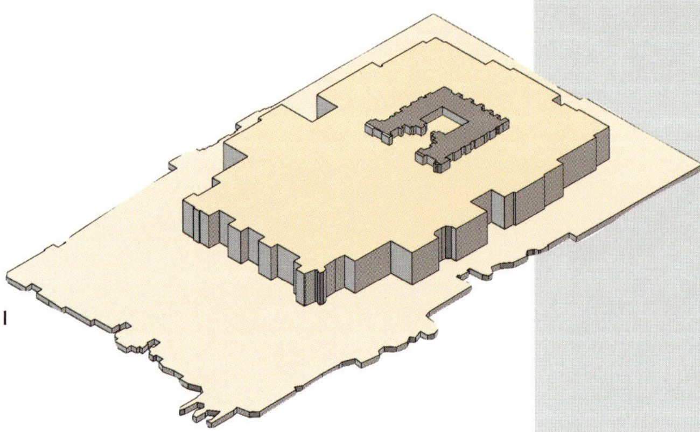
1

4 ►

1: The tripartite division into the mundane world of humans, the sacred realms of the pious, and the sacrosanct abode of the divine is expressed by the dissociation from ground at different levels.

2: The free-standing main temple becomes the primary ordering element in the overall scheme with the scooped-out sub-spaces on the rock face as supporting areas.

3: On a smaller scale, the cella becomes the focus of the arrangement of sub-shrines at the upper levels.

4: The schema of the precinct responds to organizational parameters at different levels–major and minor axes as well as hierarchy by form, placement and size. These parameters are treated differently both at macro as well as micro scales–a manifestation of the notion of centre and sub-centres.

The Kailash Temple is organized around the schema of centre and sub-centres. This notion is physically translated through the circulation path where each sub-centre becomes a 'pause point,' as a punctuation in the movement route, helping to orient oneself in the campus. Visual frames further guide the circulation. One frame leads on to the other in a smooth transition but with emphasized expression (in the form of a detail or special element at appropriate locations) at these sub-centres. This results in the perception of the schema as an episodic experience–a transition from one punctuation to the other with the significance of each being expressed by the intensity of pause. The Kailash Temple at Ellora, thus, manifests the overlay of the narrative dimension as an added communication over the experiential aspect of space, where the participating components themselves provide visual clues so as to guide one through the discovery of the parts which constitute the ensemble.

1: The organization consists of various centres: first at the entry threshold, the second at the primary baffle and then going around the threshold after climbing the secondary flights of stairs, along the axis to the meeting places and finally to the enclosure with the deity. The axial distribution from the meeting places to the sub-spaces along the same axis with the sub-deities all reinforce each other and help in mantaining the climax throughout so that even when all is seen, the effect is not diminished.

2: Miniature style painting showing the various realms and elements which come together to orchestrate the gestalt at Kailash Temple, Ellora.

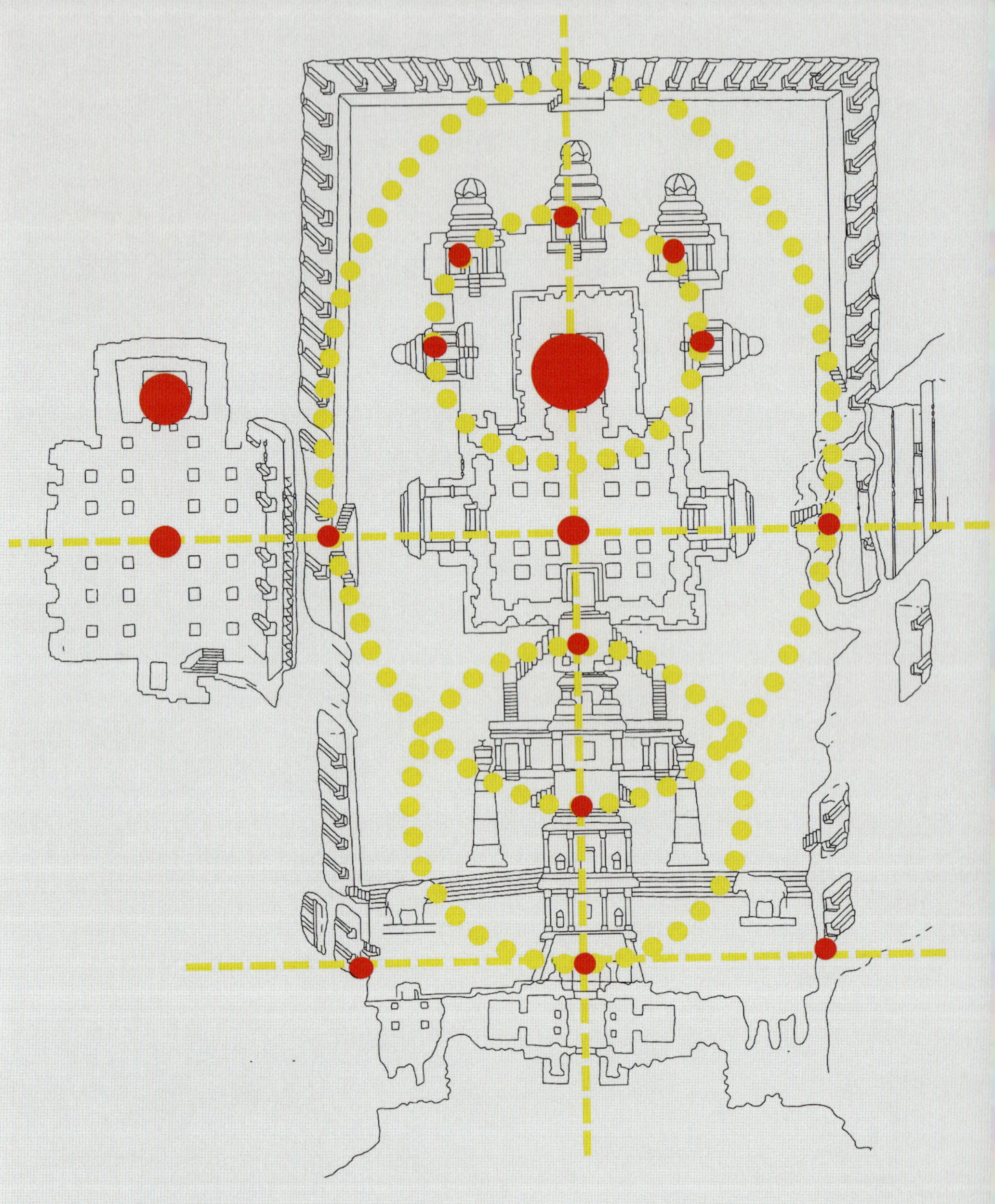

1

2 ►

This technique of gradually unfolding the spaces, episodically leading onto each other and thereby directing movement, orchestrates the experience of the space. The personalized associative decoding of the inbuilt visual clues firmly integrates the visitor with the total environment, thus fusing the perceiver and the perceived into one symbiotic existence.

At first glimpse, from outside, the temple precinct portrays itself as a forbiddingly blank wall, set within the tall rock-face seen behind, a formidable protector of the sacred realm. A proportionally small doorway, set within the flat planar surface dividing the two volumes, provides access into the complex for the interested visitor. The doorway is, by itself, a plastically treated two-storeyed mass with carved out spaces for resting or storage on the ground floor and viewing pavilions on the upper floor. These transform it into a sub-space in itself, instead of being just a plane dividing two volumes. The facade of this gateway is replete with sculpted figures and grotesques.

A vertical plane, the structural base of the Nandi bull shrine above, arrests the visual axis from the entry. Embellished with a bas-relief panel depicting the Goddess Lakshmi, it is further contained by the overhead plane of the bridge. This richly carved panel is perfectly framed by the doorway and completely occupies the visual frame. The single-storey vertical plane, slightly raised base plane and low height overhead plane, through the constricted volume together combine to make the entrance into the precinct subtle. It introduces the visitor into the scheme without announcing the grandeur of the experience to come. The entries to the scheme, on both sides, are flanked by towering figures of the *dwarapalas*–gate-keepers. This entrance volume with the intended decision of change in direction becomes a pause point, a reorientation spot from where the journey resumes after a break.

The ritual of *pradakshina* or circumambulation leads the visitor to the left, opening up the vista of large courts formed by cutting vertical faces into the rock. The courts also define the excavated temple masses from the rest of the rock mass. Facing the scooped-out shrine in the rock-face one is visually guided by the excavated and exquisitely carved elephant accentuating the diversity in rock cut treatments in the precinct. Further down, a shrine, dedicated to the River Goddess, also gives symbolic reference to the ablutional purification of oneself before entering the sacred realm of God. The visual frame, thus set up by the rough hewn and high rock-faces on the left and front along with the free-standing, finished sculpture of the elephant on the right, creates an enclosure, directly leading the eye onto the dark, unlit spaces of the shrine. This is also due to the stark contrast in an otherwise uniform view of similar material bathed in light. This forms the second point of pause and reorientation, a spatial node which offers a choice of further routes of exploration and movement.

Moving further towards the shrine, perpendicular to the entrance axis, the space to the side of the free-standing main temple is revealed, the diagonal line of sight stretching all the way to the rear of the sheer scooped-out enclosure. This spectacular view and release of space from the otherwise enclosed environment invites exploration and, with the variety of visual information, becomes the most expansive view of the precinct from within. This direction of movement is further reinforced by the wide flight of low steps inviting ascent, which segregates the temple proper from the entrance sequence, forming a low plinth. A datum, which also supports other free-standing elements like monolithic and decorative pillars or obelisks. From this plinth, three alternative routes take off, one leading to the caves in the rock-face, one to the rear of the precinct, towards the circumambulatory route, and the third to the upper levels of the main temple.

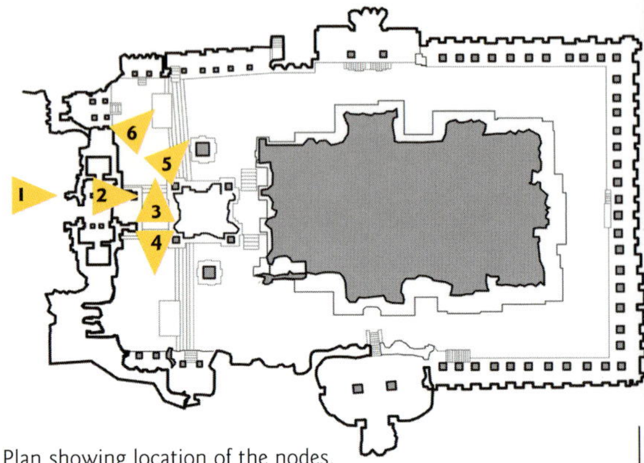

Plan showing location of the nodes.

1

2▼

1: Dressed facade and the puncture marking the only entry from the distance.

2: Low ceiling and a baffle wall across defining the transition node with the *dwarapalas*–gate-keepers–flanking the entry.

3 and 4: *Yagnashala*, space for rituals, and shrine of the River Goddess reveal themselves as the next immediate destinations, respectively to left and right of the arrival node.
Photo courtesy 1, 2 & 3: Dilip Karpoor

5 and 6: Obelisk and sculpture of an elephant forming an entry-way and framing the shrine across in the circumambulatory.

3

4

5

6

The path upstairs into the rock caves, through the narrow stairway scooped out of rock, takes the visitor past the finely finished and elaborately detailed pillars as well as rough-hewn surfaces of the rock face; from brightly lit peripheral volumes to dark, interior spaces. A journey of mystery, fantasy and surprise. This scooped-out volume is extensive, almost identical to the mass and volume of the excavated main temple mass, except that it is dedicated to a different form of the main deity.

The second route leading towards the rear of the temple is a narrow open-to-sky pathway, enclosed by the base of the temple on one side and a rhythmic arrangement of carved columns at the base of the rock-face on the other. These columns screen a well ordered (rock-cut) corridor with a multitude of sub-shrines to minor deities. This consistent pattern of open and closed, solid and void, light and dark reinforces the pulsating rhythm of the experience of the space, animating this otherwise passive part of the precinct. The overhang projecting from the columns coalesces a dynamic balance as it, while perceived from below, appears tremendously light and, while viewed from outside, unfolds the gravity-defying mass above.

7: Open-to-sky pathway around the main shrine, top lit and held by massive planes of rock.

8: Circumambulatory as colonnade scooped out of the solid rock along the periphery.
Photo courtesy: Dilip Karpoor

9: Solid mass relieved through cut-out and bridging element. This and the steps provide a frame marking the access point to reach the upper level.

10: The access point to the upper level accentuated by projection from the facade of the superstructure.
Photo courtesy: Dilip Karpoor

◄8

7

9

▼10

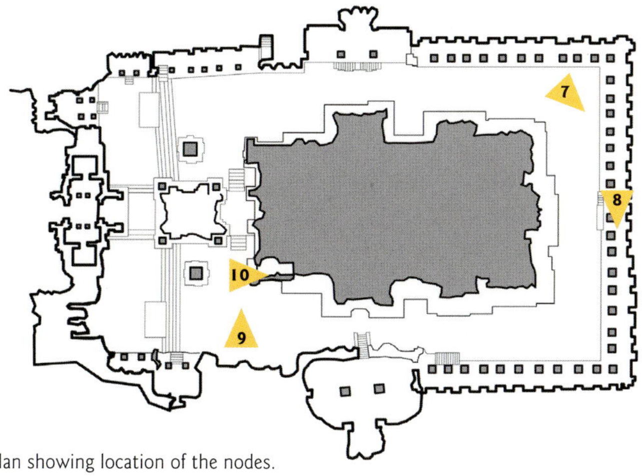

Plan showing location of the nodes.

The third route, through the doorway at the base of the main temple, leads up a narrow flight of stairs and connects the external plinth to a small pavilion at the upper level. This ascent articulates the transition from the worldly to the sacred realms of the precinct. The entire upper level of the temple is arranged as a series of ascending horizontal planes, from the Nandi shrine up to the sanctum, with minor increments in levels, further expressing the transition to the heavens. A threshold accentuates each change in level. The Nandi shrine is a free-standing mass, housing the statue of the sacred bull, the deity's vehicle.

The main temple itself comprises a hall which is divided into sub-spaces by an arrangement of quartet piers, within the central square bay, which is covered by a shallow dome and two side bays with projecting balconies, overlooking the passage outside. This space with its subtle diffused lighting gives way to the axially placed *garbhagriha*, the dimly-lit sanctum containing the idol of the deity, the culmination of sanctity in the progression of the sequence. From here, the space is directed heavenwards in the upward sweep of the *shikhara*, a pyramidal construction with embellishment, over the sanctum. Comprised of a number of miniature *shikharas* further divisible into smaller motifs, diminishing in size with the ascent, it is capped by a finial *kalash*–a keystone above the *shikhara* in the form of a ritualistic urn. This biaxial arrangement, of the horizontal and the vertical fused at the sanctum, is characteristic of Hindu temple architecture.

Although the main processional route seemingly culminates at the sanctum, a smaller secondary route takes the visitor round the sanctum at the upper level along an open-to-sky path connecting five sub-shrines housing varied forms of the main deity, each capped with smaller *shikharas* and sitting on smaller plinths. This route loops back and returns to the exit, completing the circuit and offering further choices of sub-routes. This circuitous route determines the sequential overlapping of the visual and spatial experiences of the scheme; an interactive and exploratory dialogue is set up between the visitor and the space, vitalising the entire journey with its experiential variety and vibrancy.

11

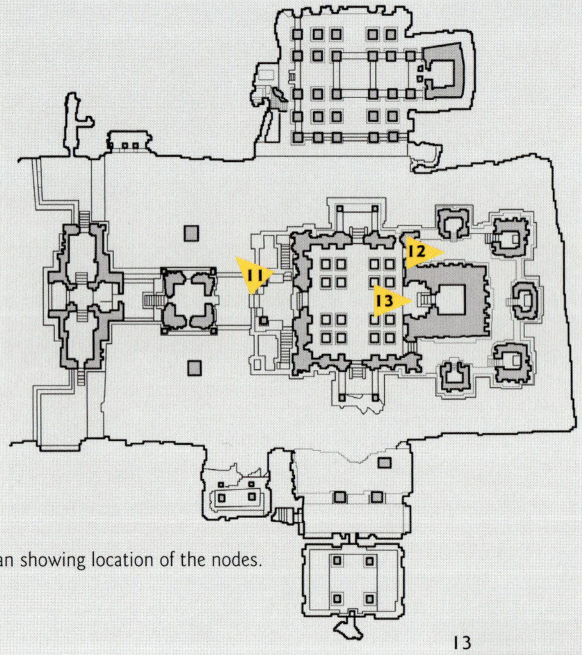

Plan showing location of the nodes.

12

14 ►

13

11: Stairway leads into an arrival pavilion framing and leading to the main shrine.

12: Sub-shrines become the focus along the circumambulatory around the main shrine. Photo courtesy: Dilip Karpoor

13: The innermost cella as a dark intimate space. Photo courtesy: Dilip Karpoor

14: Vignettes as framed at key nodal points in the campus along the movement path such as arrival (a), baffle (b), levels indicating thresholds (c,d,e), circumambulatory path (f,g), the main shrine (h) and subshrine in innermost ring (i).

d

e

c

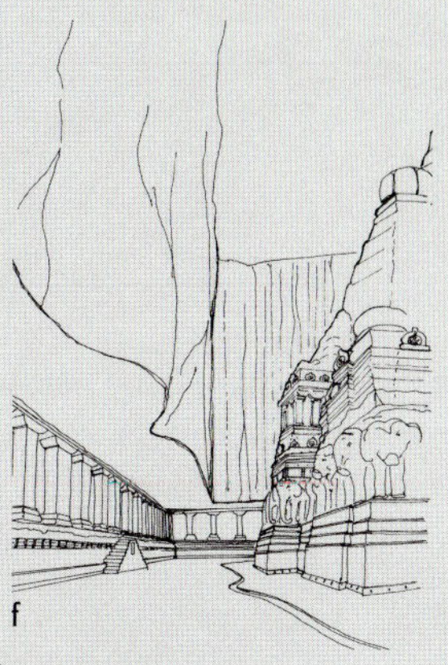

f

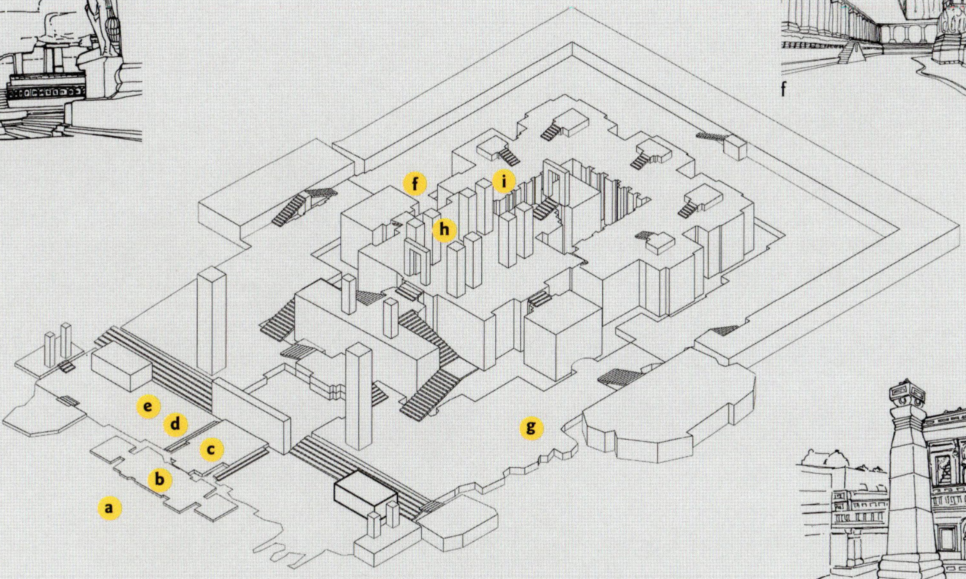

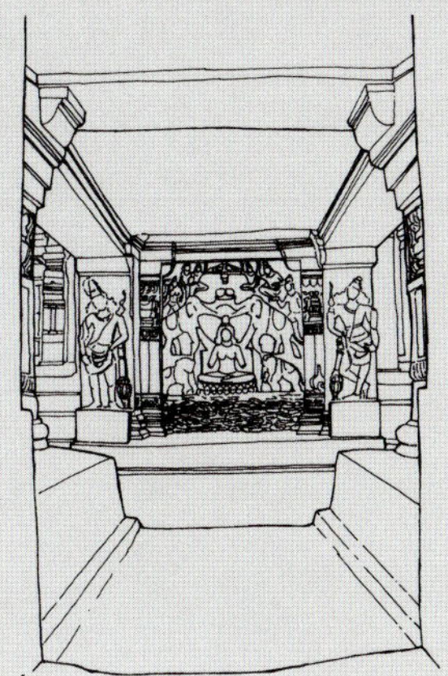

b

g

a

i

h

Thresholds

The temple exemplifies the notion of transition both in the tangible as well as the intangible realms through the sensorial and spiritual overlays. In terms of external mass, horizontal expanse of public spaces transform to vertically-extended sacred spaces. This is opposed to the inner volumes where larger and more transparent collective spaces diminish in size and scale to form the intimate and closed cellule. The rising plinth detaches the person from the earthly realm and expresses the ascent to the sacred. The transparent clarity and extroverted brightness of the open peripheral areas transform gradually into dimmer and serenely introverted indoor spaces culminating in the mysterious, dark and centric space of the sanctum.

Entry from the corporeal world through a scaled entrance with baffle wall to expose the surroundings first, circumambulatory route and subsequent entry through the ascending of steps into the procession through the collective spaces and into the final cella.

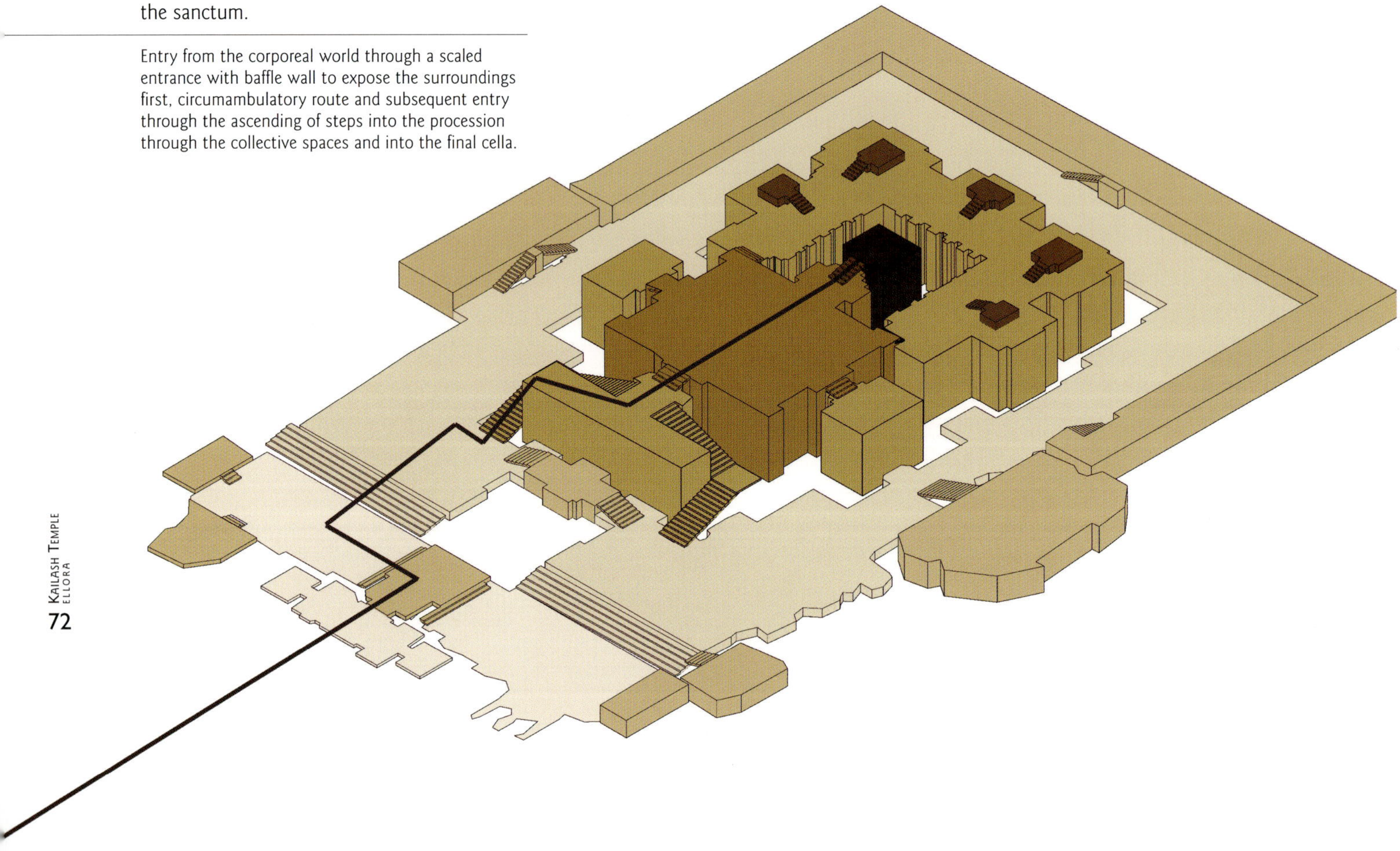

Elevation

Section

1: Opposites as counterpoints–built and unbuilt, finished and rough, light and dark, free-standing and rock-cut all co-exist, mutually enhancing perception of each other.

2 and 3: Raw and finished, free-standing and scooped out, light and dark juxtaposed together to achieve variety through diversity.

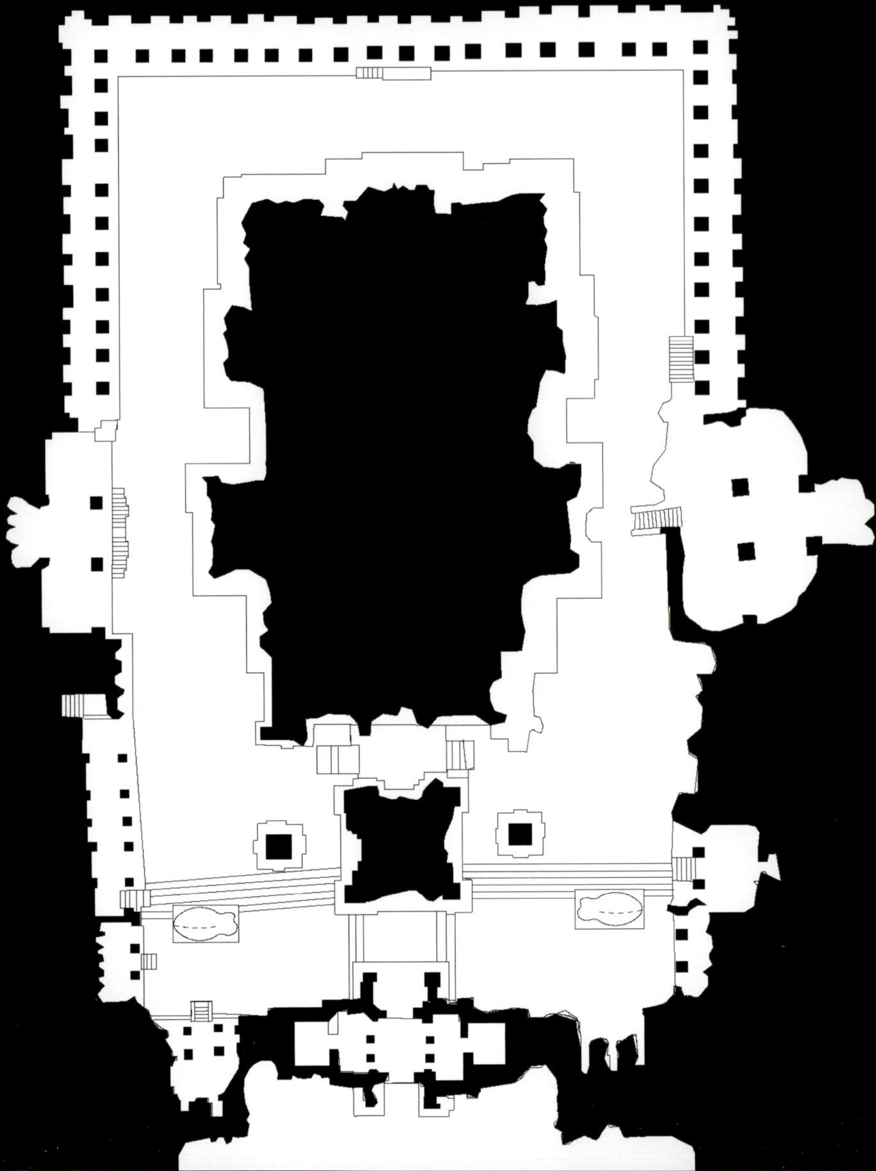

Notions

The Kailash Temple, a culmination resulting from years of building in the art of rock-cutting and heralding the glory of the patron royalty, is a fantastic fusion of technique, technology, design sensibility and socio-religious philosophy. The manner of execution, craftsmanship details, realization of the potential of the material, the influences of history and the notional sensibilities of the day are all fused together in this jewel of Indian architecture. Apart from the spatial configuration of the complex, there are a number of other aspects, which make the Kailash Temple such a masterpiece. The carved-out rough-hewn treatment of the rock-cut portions of the temple precinct as juxtaposed against portions of plastically-handled, extremely-finished and finely-treated segments of the free-standing elements set up a striking contrast. The two ways of treating the same material is a manifestation of the notions of variety and duality. This variation of textures engages also the sense of touch apart from its visual richness to elevate the ensemble into a sensorially rich experience. The sub-spaces hewn from the rock recall the primordial cave, the abode of God deep in the underbelly of the earth, as opposed to the free-standing temple with the *shikhara* with multiple replicas of smaller temples diminishing in size as they ascend. Both the nether world, inside the earth, and the mountaintop are notionally considered the abode of the gods and divine beings. The abodes contrasting in origin but essentially similar in spatial organization emphasize co-existence in apparent conflict.

Space-making through the usage of such techniques, moreover, also presents one with a diverse variety of spaces physically: of enclosure and exposure, of inside and outside, of introverted and extroverted, giving rise to different sets of connotations made evident by the treatment of these spaces. The rock-cut sub-spaces on the rock-face as well as the seemingly open-to-sky ambulatory path are essentially of the same origin, but of different spatial qualities which therefore make a visitor react differently to the space. The contradiction of the solid mass of the free-standing temple opposed to the void of the trenches around it; subtler finishes of the punched openings in the rock-face as opposed to the sheer rock of the walled enclosure; the vertical axis of the *shikhara* against the horizontal spread of the precinct etc. set up other contrasting spatialities.

Another significant aspect in this temple complex is the manner and use of light as a perceptive tool in the understanding of forms. The free-standing elements awash with sunlight, with every detail seen starkly and in totality, are in abject refutal of the deep dark and mysterious innards of the cavernous chambers. The evident clarity of forms in the open-to-sky spaces assists immediate appreciation of form and proportion while the obfuscative dimness of the caves leaves things to speculative perception and imagination. Thus the temple complex not only engages all the senses in its appreciation, but also stimulates the psyche and the mind.

Pages 76-77: Imposing ensemble replete with dualities between the built and unbuilt, dark and bright, finished and raw.

◄ 1

◄ 2

◄ 3

SUN TEMPLE
MODHERA

◄ The *kund*, stepped tank, as seen through the *torana* or gateway.

► Miniature style painting depicting the hierarchical order of the temple complex.

The Context

The Sun Temple at Modhera stands testimony to the architectural genius of bygone millennia which shaped and evolved temple building to a refined resolution. The temple complex, built in 1026-27, during the reign of Bhima I of the Solanki dynasty, is characteristic of the architectural creations of Gujarat of that period. Consisting of typical North Indian temple forms and elements, this complex is unique because of the *kund* or water tank– a subterranean architectural typology unique to this region, seen here in its most elaborate manifestation.

Dedicated to the Sun God, the ensemble is composed of three parts: the temple proper, the colonnaded hall and the *kund*. All of them share the same east-west oriented axis and face the east, towards the rising sun, to let the first rays of the Equinox sun strike the idol in the *garbhagriha*, the sanctum. The temple and the *mandapa* or pavilion are situated on a raised plinth while the *kund* is on a lower plane, and connected to the hall along the common axis by a contiguous and ascending flight of steps flanked by a ceremonial archway, the *torana*.

View from across the *kund* or tank with a shrine in the foreground against the backdrop of the steps and the temple.

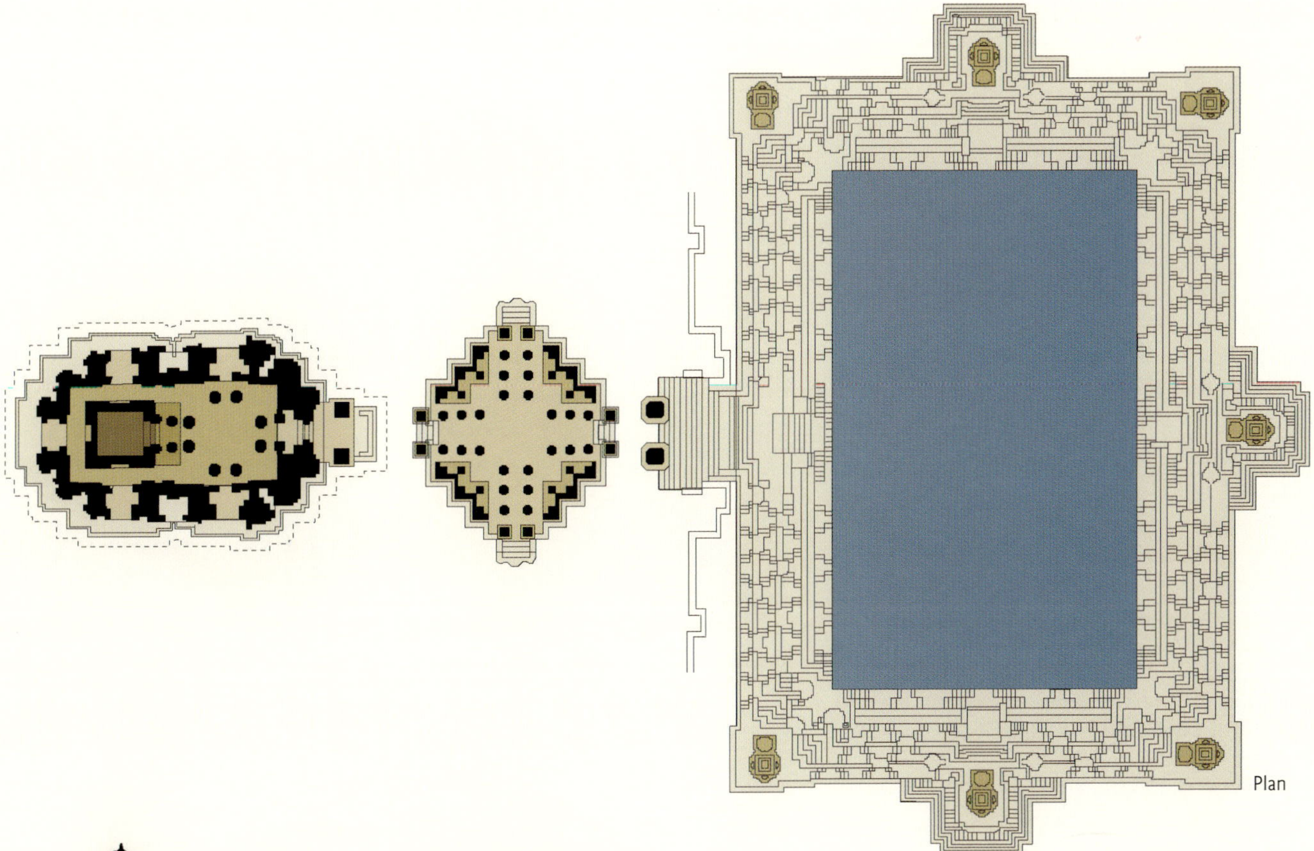

Plan

Section

THE CONSTRUCT

The *kund*, a large rectangular water tank forming the first part of the spatial sequence, shares its shorter axis with the rest of the scheme, accepting its overall order but simultaneously expressing its difference from the sacred precincts of the temple with its main axis at right angles to it. A geometric composition of steep steps and platforms elaborately arranged and leading circuitously down to the water, the *kund* is interspersed and punctuated by sub-shrines of almost 60 minor deities. The inverted pyramid formed by the steep angle of the steps descending to the water is strongly complemented by the identical profile of the *shikhara* of the temple rising into the sky, forming a straight line-of-sight, mirroring the roof-forms in the water in a symbolic unification. The *kund* and temple manifest a harmonious relationship, though mutually contrasting. The *kund* becomes an altar to water while the temple is a shrine to the sun, an embodiment of fire. This is a personification of the Vedic myth that the sun emanates from the dark inert of a primordial ocean, as well as the notion of duality and contradictory co-existence.

The entrance arch, the *torana*, with a trabeated assembly of multi-faceted sculpted columns, ornate cross beams and carved flying arches, is customised in the regional style and resembles the *toranas* at nearby regions of Siddhpur or Vadnagar. The temple sits on a classical decorative high plinth, the *kharashila pitha*, with a brick infill and stone facing, embellished with elaborate mouldings and string courses. This plinth further articulates the difference between the sacred realm of the temple and the profane world of human ablutions. The main route into the temple, as implied by the organization, is down into the *kund* and, after ablutions, climbing up, ascending towards the heavens, through the *torana*, thereby symbolizing the ritual purification of the person before entering the precincts of God.

1

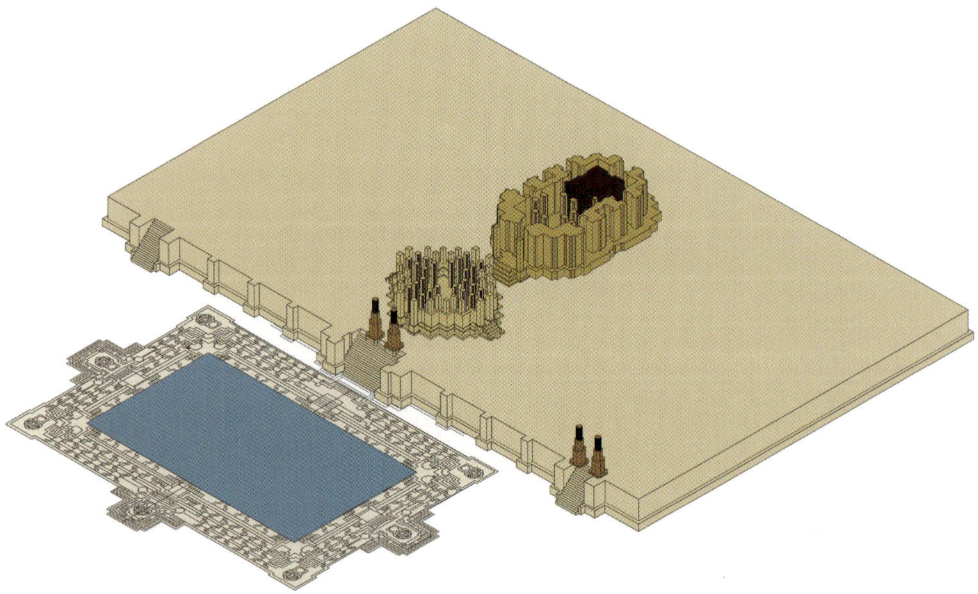

2

The *torana* leads onto the *sabha mandapa*, a square pavilion measuring 50 square metres, placed diagonally with the organizational axis of the scheme, the corners becoming the entries facing the cardinal directions. A pair of free-standing columns flank each entrance and an aisle formed by a double row of similar columns links them to the inner space, intersecting in the centre leaving an octagonal space which is covered by a shallow dome, four metres from the floor and rising to seven metres. A half height dwarf wall with a sloping back-rest (*asana*) runs along the sides of the pavilion enclosing it, without obstructing the view to the outside. The space outside of the octagon is interspersed with columns creating smaller sub-spaces. However, unlike other examples typical of this style, this ornate pavilion stands detached from the penultimate hierarchy consisting of the *goodha mandapa* for devotional discourses and the ultimate inner sanctum, the *garbhagriha*–the womb-like space where the deity is housed

3

4▼

This inner sanctum of the shrine, measuring 15 metres by 24 metres is largely an enclosed volume, with rhythmically undulating and recessed wall planes, which create a variety of shadows on the outside and a variation of spaces on the inside. These modulated vertical planes are further relieved by fine window openings along strategic points on the periphery. The *mandovara*–a panelled wall face–is richly embellished with carvings and figures. These sculpted narratives in the lower dado of the wall consist of motifs of the *padma* or lotus, *karnakar* or gestures of the hand and *kirtimukha*, a composite lion-dragon architectural motif known as 'the face of glory.' The minor deities are enshrined in the smaller niches in the upper zones in their respective hierarchy, with important ones in central cardinal positions and the attendant gods on the sides.

The superstructure, although now destroyed, was marked by a pyramidical arrangement of small turrets and miniature finials with a multi-faceted tall *sekhari shikhara* in the middle. A rather peculiar aspect of the temple at Modhera is also the independent *garbhagriha*, a five-bay sanctum or *mulaprasada* enclosed within a shrine, surrounded by an ambulatory between the shrine walls. There also exists an under-ground cellar, sunk by about 3.5 metres in which stands the pedestal with the idol of Surya, the Sun God.

1: Articulation by variations in the ground plane.

2: Articulation by variations in the degree of enclosure.

3: Articulation by variations in the roof forms.

4: The complex with the main shrine, *kund* and the independent column gateways to the right.

The Realms

The complex in essence comprises three aspects–the domestic, the religious and the sacred–marking the journey from the mortal to the divine worlds, from the profane group activities to the singular oneness with the Creator through strongly delineated hierarchies. However, each part within the entire scheme, though seen as a comprehensive composition and as a single integral unit, is effectively a grouping together of individual 'wholes' and is articulated as a totality in itself, not only as a notion, but also in the manner of resolution of form and function. Thus, notwithstanding the perception of the three units simultaneously, the *kund* as the ablution and domestic centre, the *mandapa* as the sacred gathering space, and the temple as the abode of the gods are, by themselves, complete architectural entities. They are connected together by visual juxtaposition and adjacency as well as the organizational axis and the implied route of movement. This manner of articulation and inherent contradiction, with each element simultaneously being a part of a bigger scheme and also a whole in itself, is an expression of the religious-philosophic notion of worlds within worlds, of the Atman and the Brahman. The infinitesimal and infinity are mutually interdependent and yet complete by themselves.

1: Looking through the side entrances across to catch a glimpse of the main shrine.

2: The various individual realms within the same complex. **a**: The *kund*–worldly, open, public; **b**: the pavilion–social, semi-enclosed, group; **c**: the sanctum–sacred, enclosed, individual.

1

2 ►

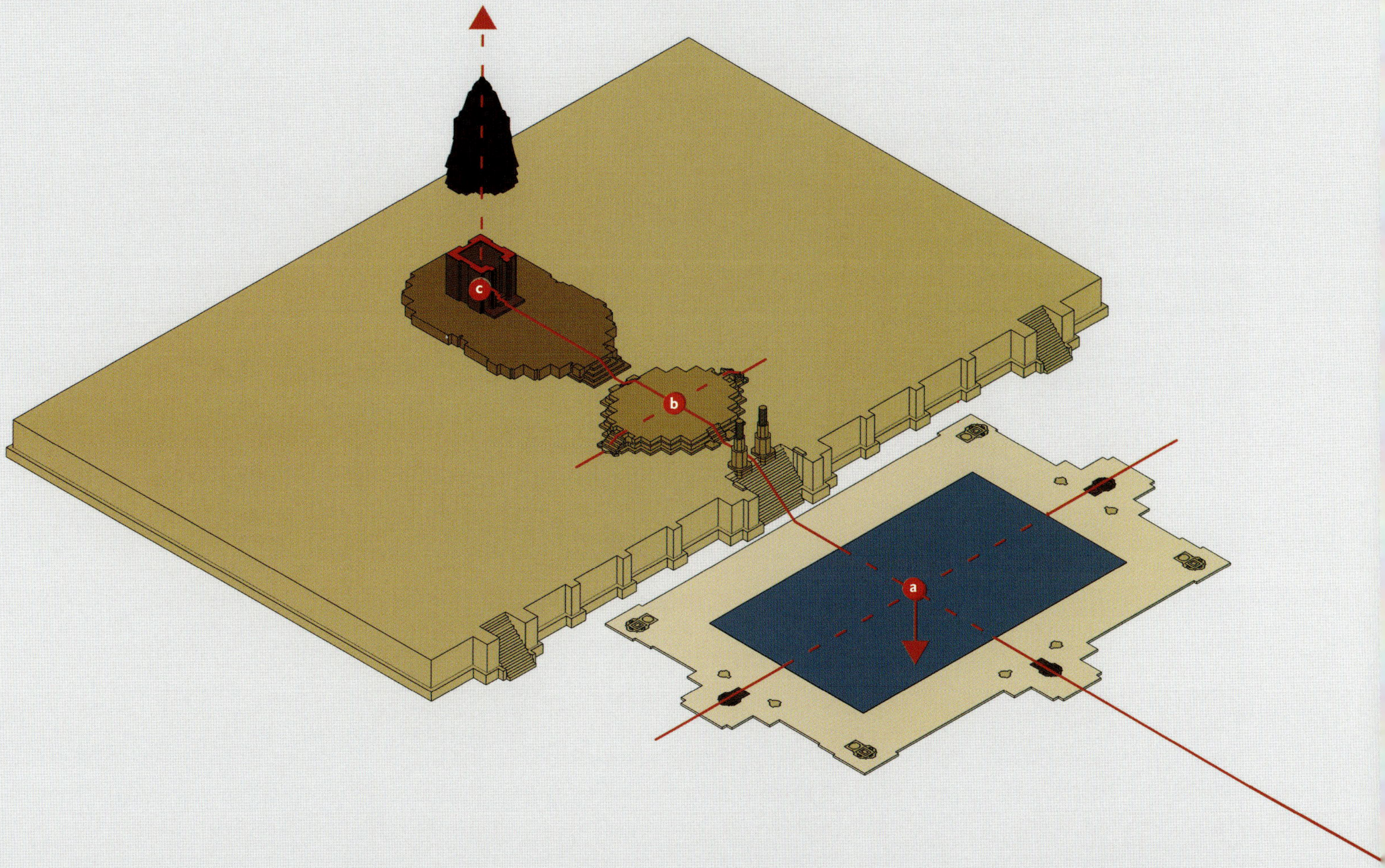
c
b
a

The temple complex is perceived as a unified composition along a single axis. However, the ritual and circulation route, which determines the movement through the space, guides the experience of the precinct, seen as a sequential overlapping of a series of visual frames. This results in an animated and episodic unfolding of the intricacies of the ensemble rather than an expansive one-time registration of the overall complex. The arrival to the complex is along the axis of its orientation, which offers in the visual frame from a distance only the outline of the *shikhara* of the temple, the flat facade of the *mandapa* and temple base seemingly fused into one elevation. This frame is more or less two-dimensional, refuting the impression of the temple being composed of two or more parts, and with the eye being guided skyward by the profile of the *shikhara*.

1: Miniature study juxtaposing the visual axis with the movement path at the Modhera Sun Temple.

2: Vignettes framed as one moves about from node to node at the Sun Temple–arrival node (a), *kund* (b), circumambulatory (c), final ascent (d), and the sequences within (e,f,g).

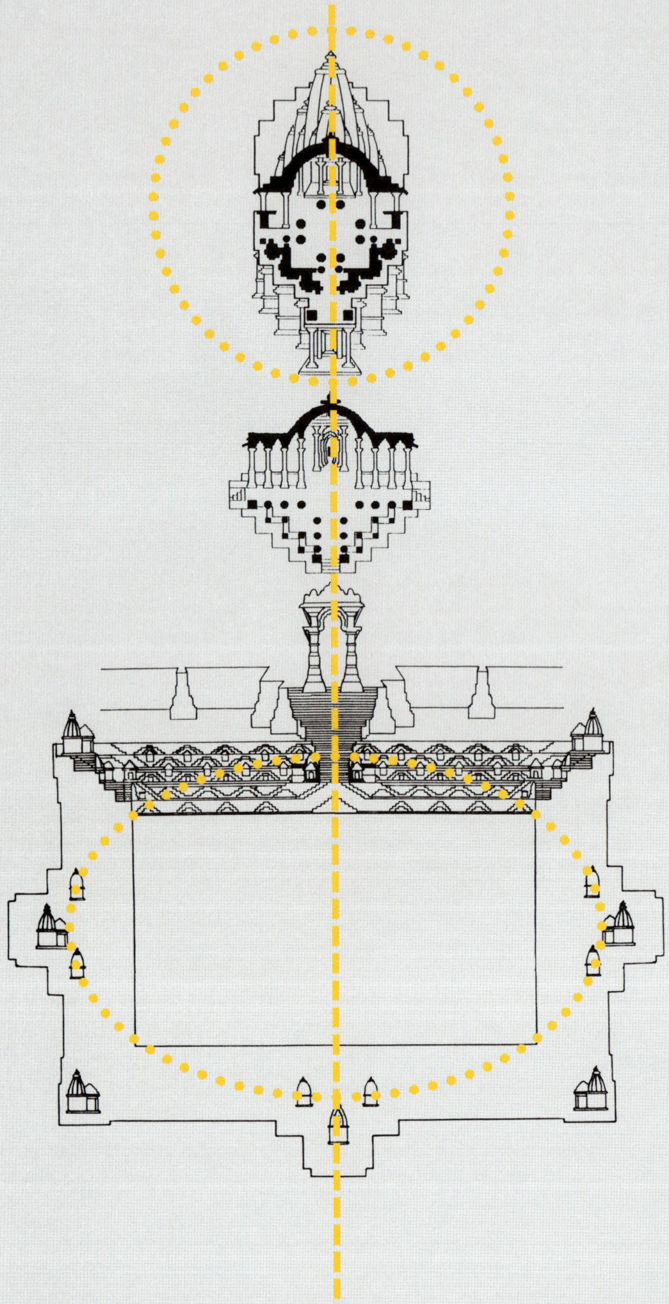

1 2 ►

g
f
e
d
b
a

As one draws nearer the temple along the axis, the foreground of the *kund*, begins to register in the visual frame, the eye being deflected downwards by the ever-growing profusion of visual information of steps and platforms interspersed with sculptured shrines. The vertical thrust of the *shikhara* is countered by the horizontal expanse of the *kund*, which has its longer axis perpendicular to the organizational axis of the scheme. This is balanced within the builtform by the perspectival arrangement of columns, roof lines and elements, thereby also implying visual depth. These three axes, set up by the rising *shikhara*, spreading *kund* and penetrating perspectives of columns, strike a dynamic balance, setting up a forceful equilibrium.

The ritual dip in the holy water needed to cleanse oneself of earthly sins requires a descent into the *kund*. From this point, due to the steep angle of descent and the matching pitch of the roof, the mirrored image of the temple *shikhara* is seen in the water, further emphasizing the need to reach the divine after the ablution. The enclosure of the surrounding steps on all sides leaves only the temple in vision. An offshoot of the need to maintain this angle in order to achieve the reflection is that the steps do not lead directly to the water but meander sideways and downward in a serpentine route. Circumventing the water-body, one is forced to leave the axis and again rejoin it on the other side. The smaller shrines make the descent itself an event instead of reaching the water as the goal.

On the way up, the *torana*, again due to the steep angle, frames the sky and alludes to the symbolic gateway to the sacred heavens before granting access to the *mandapa*. The alternative to this descent to the water in order to get to the temple is a circumambulatory route which takes a detour around the *kund*.

1

2

1: The *kund* placed axially to the main shrine, while affording the view, diverts movement around the water-body, shifting one away from the axis for some time.

2: Movement around the *kund* gradually reveals the depth of the ensemble and orients one towards it mentally as well as physically.

3

4

This digression from the axis, however, turns the direction of vision and, thus, presents the whole precinct in perspective, for the first time giving a realization of the depth of the composition and allowing an appreciation of the forms together, which are symmetrical about the main axis. This route negotiates the plinth, which segregates the temple from the *kund* and enters the *mandapa* from the side, meeting the other route at the centre of the hall. The third route from the *kund* branches off towards the right to reach a podium after climbing a flight of steps, entering it through a free-standing *torana* and turning back to enter the *mandapa* from the opposite side. All three routes, splitting up at the *kund*, meet at the centre of the *mandapa*, and continue from there as one.

3: A widening flight of steps and a pair of columns as a *torana* mark the entry on the axial path from the *kund*.

4: Steps and entry portal along the perpendicular axis of the *nritya mandapa* or dance pavilion become an alternative entry for the movement path around the *kund*.

Plan showing nodal points.

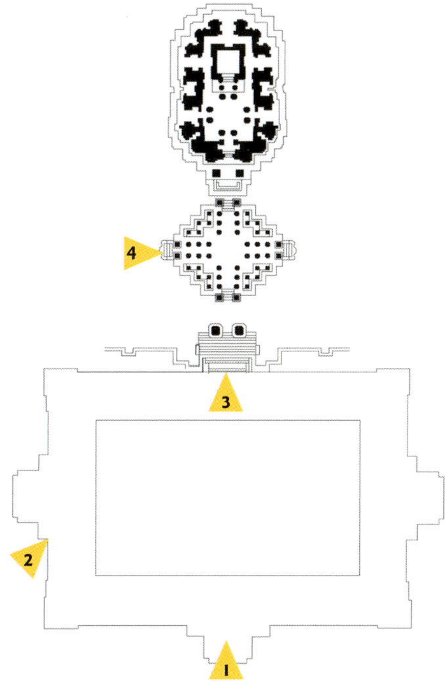

The panoramic vision of the exterior landscape, until arrested by the entry into the hall, allows appreciation of its form, proportion of massing and organization. The hall, though indoors, is well lit due to its being open on all sides. The ranges of vision here are more intimate, within a few feet and, therefore, the details, elements and treatment can be appreciated. The *mandapa*, being perfectly symmetrical on both axes, gives identical frames of view out into the landscape on three sides, with one side opening out into the *kund* and the fourth side leading onto the temple. The *mandapa* itself sits on a small plinth, raising it above the surrounding ground. The route to the temple leads out of the *mandapa* through the colonnaded exit with a decorative archway, typical of architecture of the region, back to the ground level outside. A small distance of open-to-sky space separates it from the entrance porch of the temple, thereby articulating the detachment of the two structures, not far enough to feel scattered, but sufficient to emphasize separation.

Once within the temple, there are two spaces, the *goodha mandapa*, the prayer hall, and the *garbhagriha*, the sanctum, both part of the same mass externally but separated internally by a constriction of wall planes. These spaces, being completely enclosed, are dark and there is only appreciation of light and shade here, and therefore of texture. The *goodha mandapa*, lit by two windows on either side, is perceived as a group space, albeit small, due to the central volume and rising roof of the dome above. The *garbhagriha*, the abode of the deity, is dark and unlit, leaving perception to the imagination and thereby totally integrating the devotee with his conception of God. Here the appreciation is not of sensorial experience of mass, surface or texture, but of notions of understanding.

5 and 6: The detached *goodha mandapa* marks the next transition, pronounced through light falling on the entry portico and framed axially between the row of columns as perceived from the *nritya mandapa*.

5

6

7

Windows lighting the small passage sandwiched between the sanctum and the external wall draw the attention of the devotee to the *pradakshinapatha*, the ritual path of circumambulatory prayer. The visual clues only come as light and intermittent darkness. Thus, the precinct is experienced in a series of vignettes, each one leaving its imprint on the already accumulated experience of the previous spaces, disclosing the sequence in an accretive manner of sense perception. The senses are stimulated in a sustained rhythm of increasing abstraction–mass, form, elements, material, treatment, light and shade, texture and finally notion.

7: The inner circumabulatory is punctuated cardinally through light cutouts on the outer periphery.

8: The cella is dark and the final point in the movement sequence placed axially to receive the first rays of the rising sun from the east.

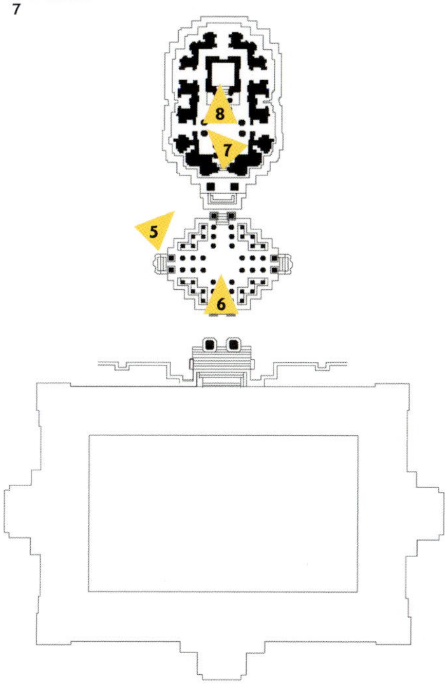

Plan showing the position of nodes.

8

The precincts embody and articulate varying senses of transition, a manifestation of the idea of continuity, a phenomenon which like time does not break but can be extended by pauses and detours to prolong the enriching experience.

These translate into the idea of the threshold, a space where one realm gives way to another in a smooth transfer instead of an abrupt disjunction. The varying degrees of enclosure are traversed from the *kund* as a completely exterior phenomenon, a landscape element, to the *mandapa*, a semi-closed, semi-open pavilion which leads onto the walled enclosure of the temple, consisting of the marginally open *goodha mandapa* and the totally closed *garbhagriha*. This variation of enclosures is accompanied by the transition in light intensity too, from the totally sunlit and bright *kund* to the moderately-lit hall leading onto the subtly lit interior hall and absolutely dark sanctum. The third overlay to these variations is the interpretative understandings of sanctity, from the profane and domestic realm of ablutions at the *kund* to the cleansed gathering hall to the sanctified inner hall and the sacrosanct cella. All these are achieved architecturally with the help of the entire palette available: from the usage of site in terms of placement, orientation and the creation of levels to the proportions of the superstructure. The massing and the kind of entablature, the carvings and the overlays of symbols are all bathed with expert sensitivity and knowledge of the quality of light falling on each of these.

Thus, the precinct interweaves and embodies diverse interpretations of the journey. The route from a particular space to a destination overlaid with meaning and reinforced by the form, as seen in the sectional profile of the complex, from the nether world of the *kund* to the earthly realm of the hall and then the ethereal abode of the gods.

Facing page: Sectional isometric showing the diversity in structural massing.

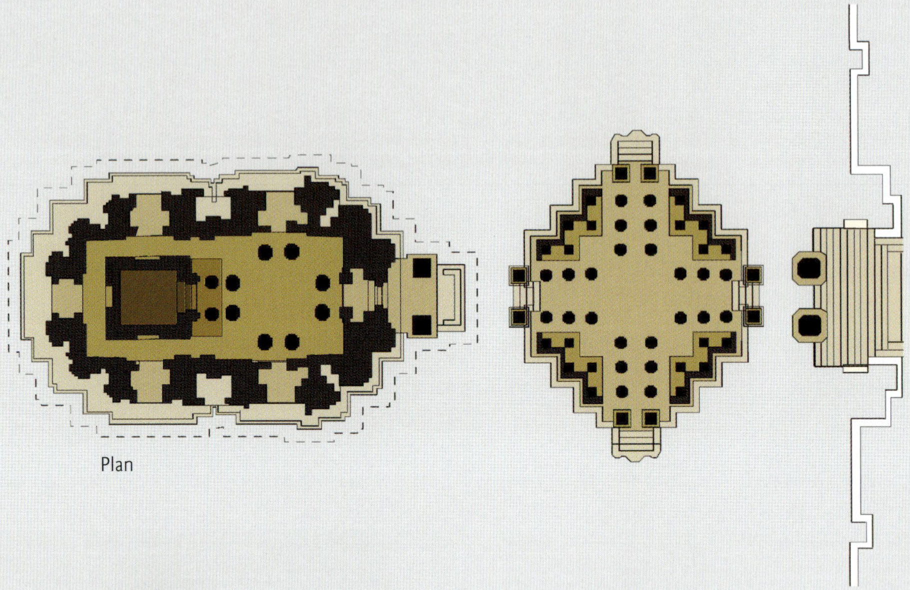

Plan

Section

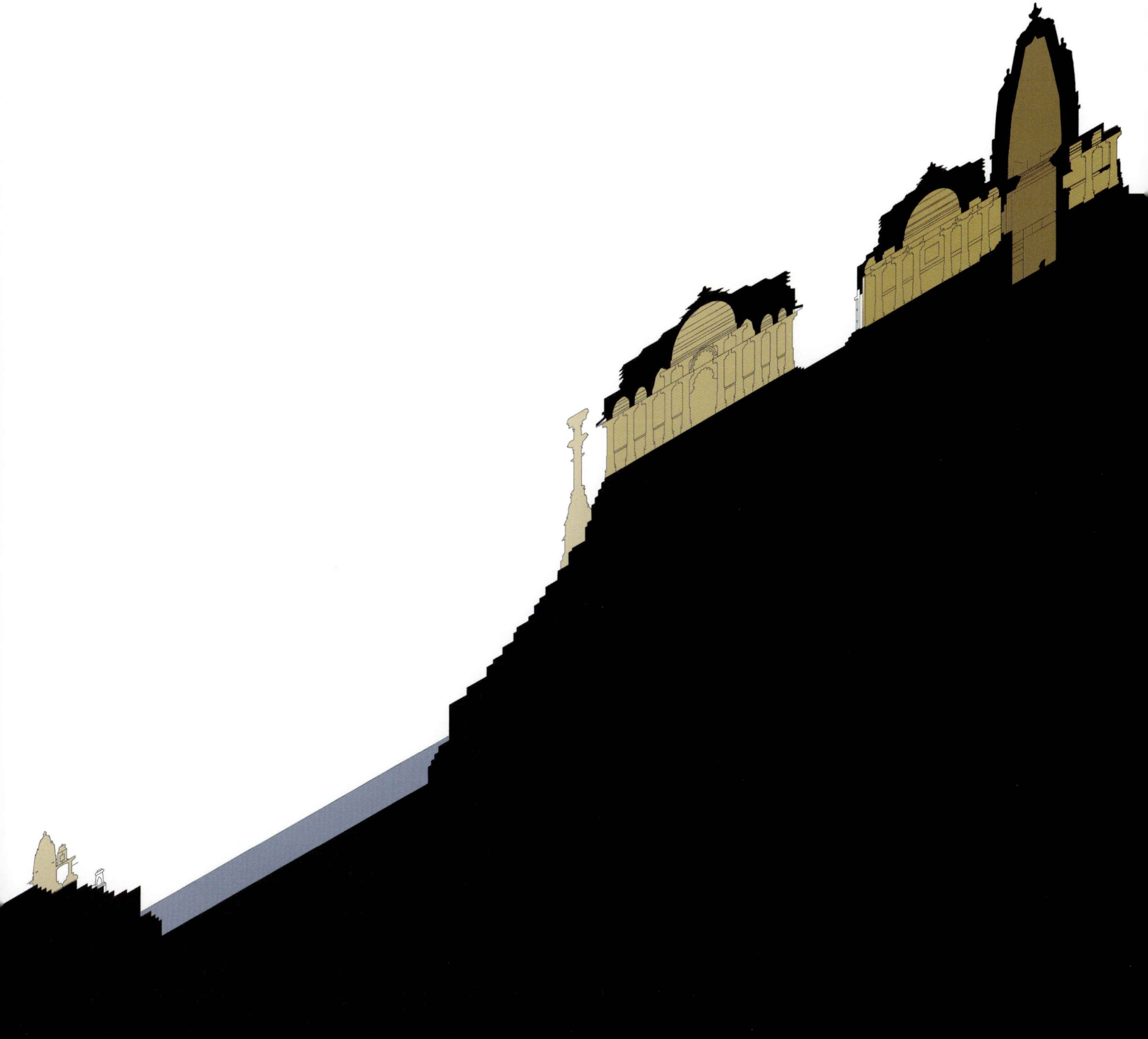

Notions

The Sun Temple at Modhera exhibits the biunity of fire and water in a highly symbolic manner. The temple is conceived as a physical manifestation of the ritual *arghya*–worshipping the sun (the sign of fire) through its counterpart, water.

The symbolic forms of fire and water–an upward and an inverted triangle–are used explicitly to reinforce this duality. Steps leading into the *kund* form an inverted triangle housing water, which reflects the upward triangle of fire, formed by the temple and *shikhara*. The *kund*, the ritual water tank, is placed on the same organizational axis of the temple representing fire but shows subtle deviations in emphasizing its identity. Mutual existence of these opposite principles is further enhanced by the interlocking pattern of triangles formed by the steps of the *kund*.

1: Miniature-style representation of the Modhera Sun Temple.

2: Notional dualities juxtaposed in the architecture through its form, scale, massing, proportioning and location.

Pages 96-97: Steps within the *kund* offering pauses and movement choices.

1 2 ►

CITY PALACE
UDAIPUR

◄ A *chhatri* at the Badi Chatursali court in the City Palace at Udaipur.

► Miniature style impression of the courts, pavilions and built mass comprising the City Palace, Udaipur.

A descendent of Bapa Rawal of the 8th century Sisodia clan and the fifty-third ruler of the Mewar dynasty, King Udaisingh II established Udaipur in the middle of the 16th century as a defence retreat.

The former capital of Mewar, Chittod, due to its easy accessibility, was quite vulnerable and thus suffered frequent attacks. Udaipur, comparatively, was found to be a safer location as it was surrounded by hills and was accessible only through a few mountain passes, which could be easily defended. The new capital of Mewar was, therefore, established at Udaipur. The royal citadel known as the City Palace was built upon natural outcrops of bedrock on the top of a hillock.

Ensconced within the fort walls and numerous gates, the City Palace campus at Udaipur overlooks the entire city on one side and is flanked on the other side by the artificially created Pichola Lake.

The citadel, built in 1559, has been occupied and functional since more than 400 years. It has continuously grown, altered and subsequently developed by over 22 Maharanas, over the past four centuries.

The city palace was divided into two distinct zones, the *mardana* and the *zenana*, for the male and female members of the royal family respectively. While the *zenana* consisted of residential quarters for the royal ladies, the *mardana* had banquet halls, reception halls, residential suites and royal offices.

The royal inheritances, cultural traditions and the architectural legacies are maintained and continued even now. Segregating the royal residences and transforming the rest into museums, libraries and hotels has made the campus and its components more accessible to visitors today.

The plaza affronting the City Palace looking towards the entrance gate.

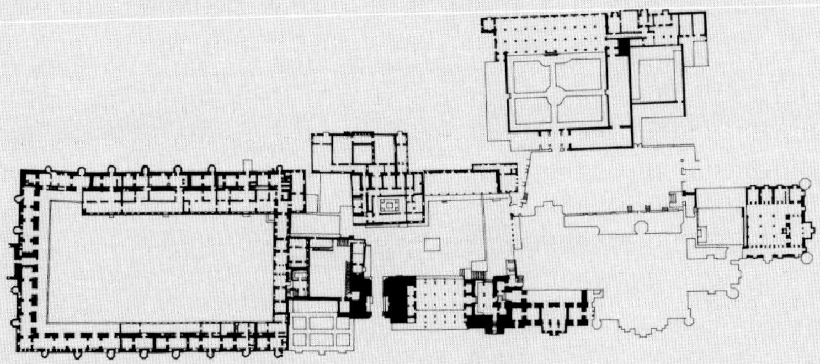

First level

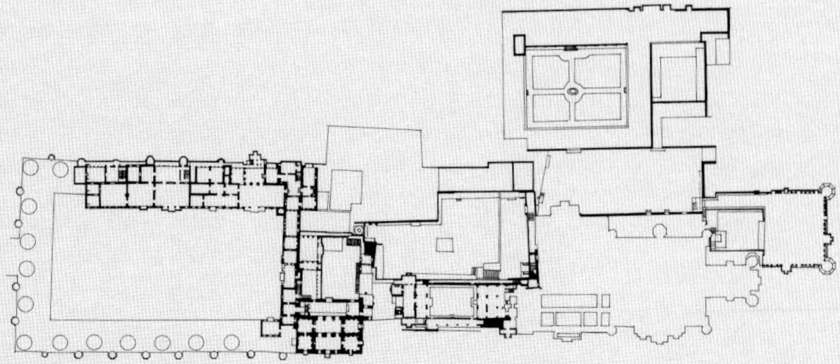

Second level

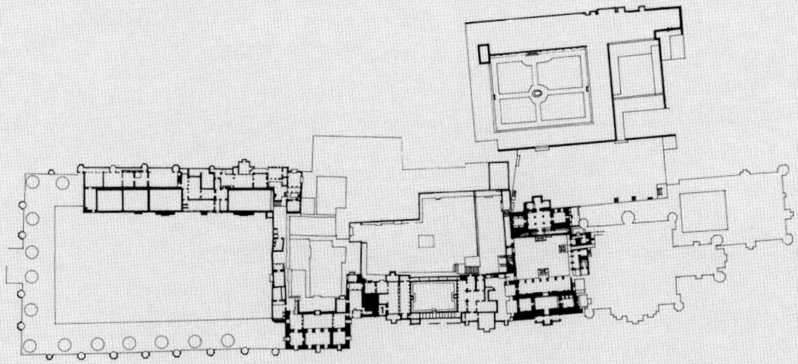

Third level

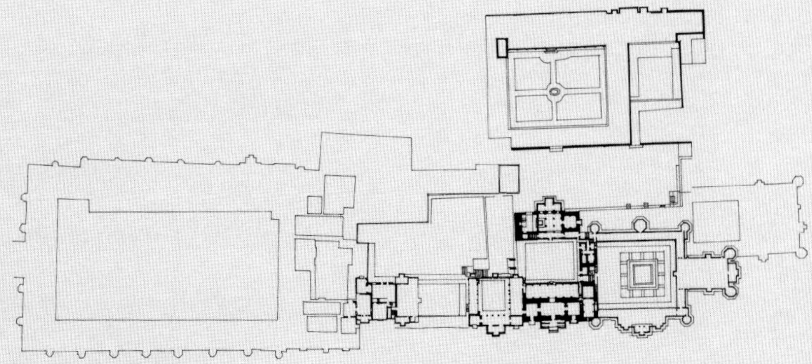

Fourth level

N

Longitudinal section

The Construct

The palace is situated on the highest peak of the city over a natural hillock for defence purposes. This hilly terrain has influenced the organization of its planning in terms of its vertical growth, distribution and expansion of spaces over a number of interconnected levels following the natural contours. These levels are connected and accessed by narrow, steep and winding stairs, which once again primarily serve the defence intentions well.

Essentially a load bearing structure in brick and stone rubble masonry, the palace has been externally cladded with slabs of sandstone. On the inside, it is finished with smooth white lime plaster. Beginning with the 16th century, it was built, accretively, over four centuries and, thus, it displays a number of stylistic variations and adaptations. While Hindu (Rajput), Islamic and Colonial (British) influences can be traced in the decor and motifs as well as spatial elements, they have blended well to emerge as a singular composite and harmonious ensemble. Whether they be the trabeated stone column-and-beam construction system, the multi-point *mayur* (peacock) shaped arches, the arcuated structure with the pointed Islamic arches or the segmental Colonial arches held by the keystone, the decor in terms of miniature style paintings on the wall, gemstone and pearl inlay, mirror mosaic or ceramic tile cladding, all elements have been held together largely through their spatial contiguity.

The super massing as seen from the entrance courtyard.

Courtyards and pavilions become key components of spatial organization in response to the harsh hot climate and the high sense of privacy. The *chhajas* (protective slabs) and *chhatris* (small pavilions) impart to the construct its Rajput identity. The built form is an intricate maze of built and unbuilt spaces, where living spaces are grouped around a number of small courtyards. Colonnaded spaces flank these courts on the ground level, while protruding balconies and *jharokhas* (projecting spaces) overlook them from the upper floors. The courtyards, thus, provide introverted yet active outdoor living spaces. The terraces become external, yet private living spaces with tall parapet walls, and *chhatris* are effectively used in the evenings and nights as they are pleasantly cool even during the harsh summers, especially due to the presence of the lake.

The *mardana*–extroverted realm for males–and the *zenana*–introverted realm for females–are two distinct zones, each complete on its own, around a courtyard with common services such as kitchens, stables and movement nodes connecting the two. A strict sense of privacy for the women folk has led to this bipartite division and the use of introverted courtyards and veiled *jharokhas* with *jali* or screen walls in the palace. Many of the external walls are also kept blank and devoid of openings in such sensitive areas of the palace.

Thus, defence (from the harsh, hot and dry climate as well as from enemies), a very high sense of privacy and heightened sense of dignity gradients (for female members and family functions for the public) have largely influenced the space organization, construction as well as articulation of the City Palace campus at Udaipur.

Miniature style painting depicting the 'leisure zones' fused together to form the ultimate paradise for the lord of the region, the king.

The Realms and Thresholds

A royal palace and citadel being a grander version of a home still retains the obligation to serve the manifold functions and activities demanded of it, more so due to strong cultural and traditional roots. It is faced with contradictory requirements such as intimate family space versus collective royal courts and banquets; royal members and dignitaries versus servants and attendants; and recreational functions versus diplomatic and formal events. In addition to these, the Rajput/Hindu customs, where women assume special honour and status while guarding their privacy, have to be accommodated. This extra emphasis on their privacy and honour restricts the movement, accessibility and visual communication to and from the women's zone.

The palace is, thus, divided primarily into two distinct realms–one for the male members and the other for the ladies–called the *mardana* and *zenana* respectively. Organized around a courtyard, these realms are self-contained. Privacy dictums make the *zenana* extremely introverted with very limited or no fenestration on the external edges. The access within is often narrow, contrived and indirect and even that, only for a limited group of visitors.

The realm for men, the *mardana* is further zoned such that the lower, and closer to ground, areas of the palace are accessible to courtiers, visitors or even commoners at times. This accessibility tapers down towards the zones at the upper level, which tend to be largely for immediate family, royal members, royal ladies and only invited guests.

The change in levels, constricted entries, indirectness of movement paths, the series of gateways and the overall opacity imply thresholds to these realms in visual terms through the excessive presence of wall planes.

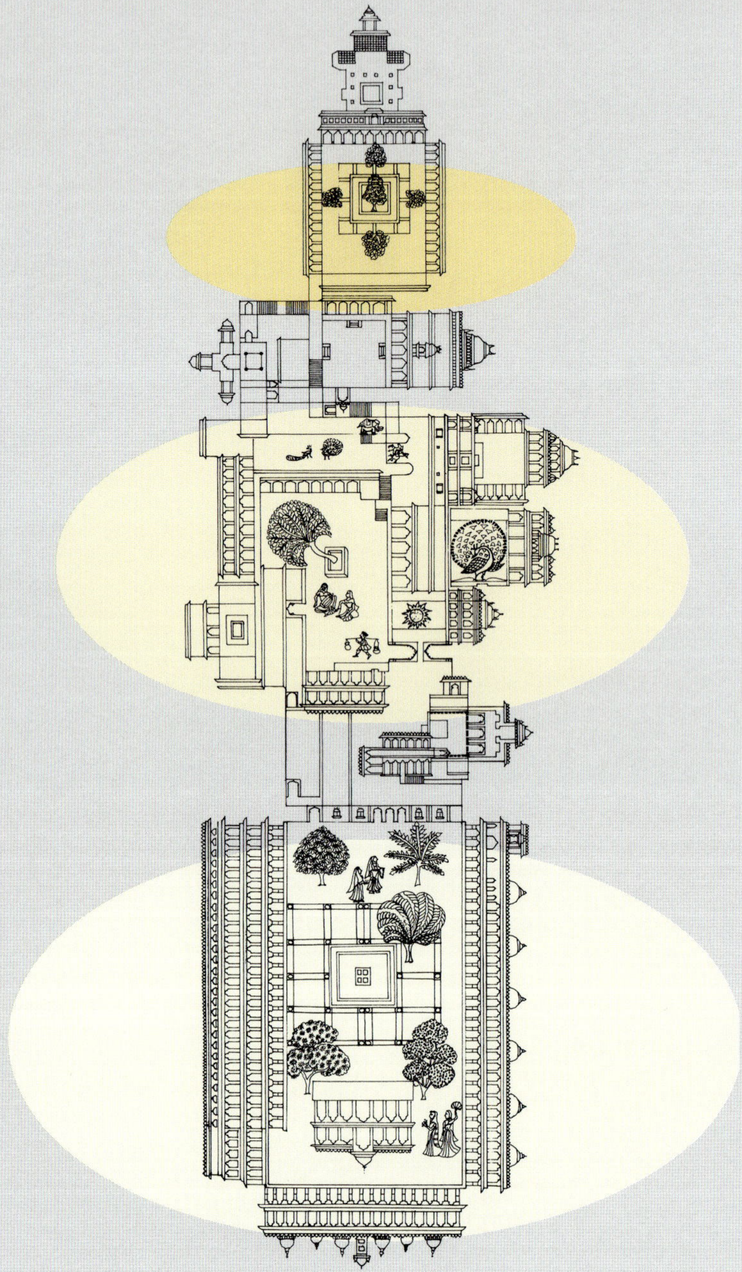

Artist's impression of the City Palace, showing the varied contrasting spaces which are tied together in an ensemble.

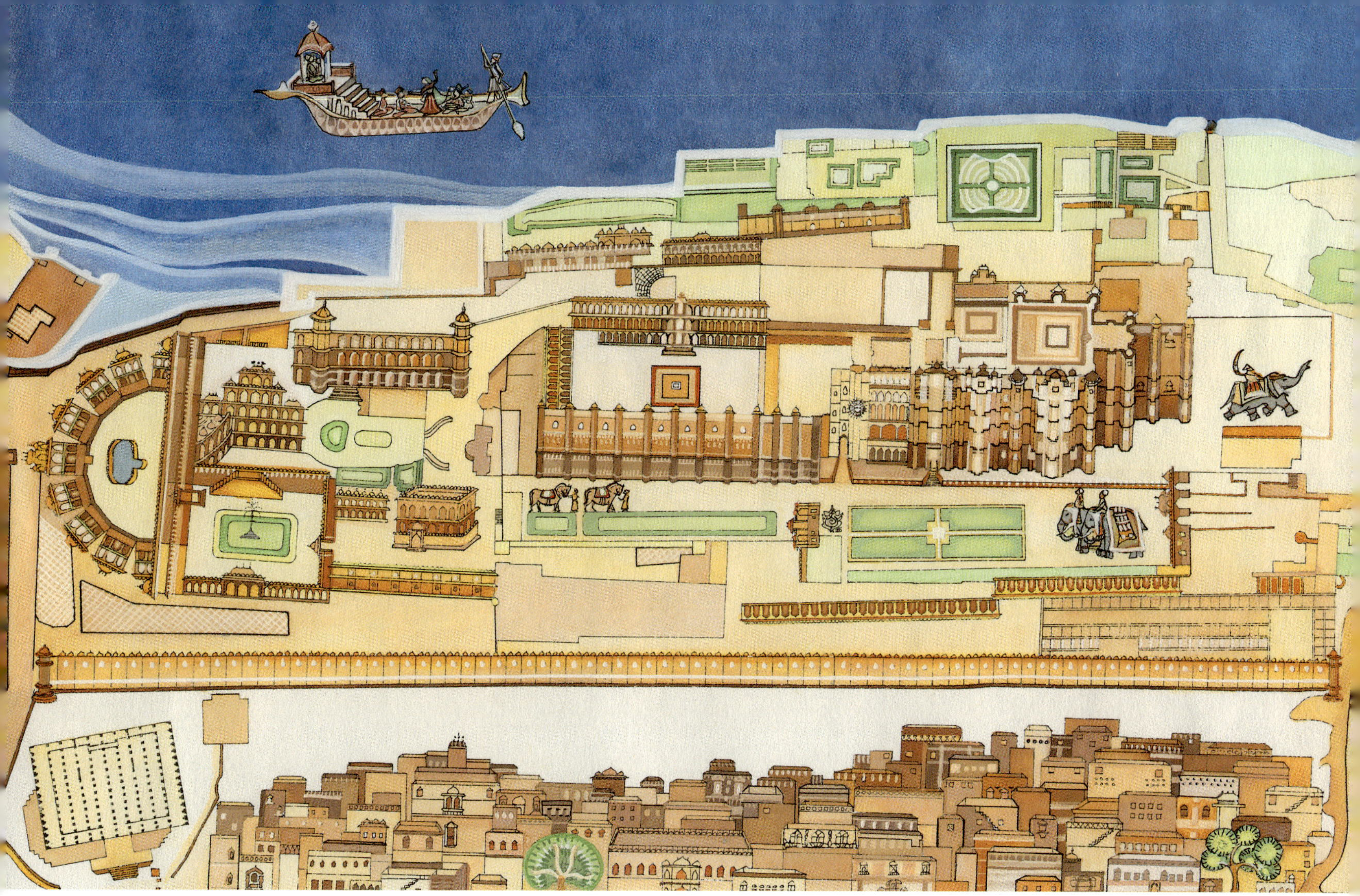

Miniature style painting showing the realms–public, private and for pleasure–with the kind of surface treatment each one receives through architectural elements.

The cupolas and *chhatris* adorning the terraces, placed as they are on the pinnacle of the hill, form the visual reference for the palace from afar. The palace is physically approached through winding paths negotiating and circumventing minor land contours of the hilly terrain. This affords glimpses of the varying skyline of the palace. The first threshold en-route is the Hathi Pol (Elephant Gate), which sites itself on the principal access route from the old city called the Jagdish Marg. This marks the first layer providing a further lead towards the royal precinct.

The access route aligning with the Jagdish temple further forms an axis to Badi Pol in the north court, which is surrounded by the built mass and a wall with eight *toranas* (arches). This forms the intermediary and buffer space between the royal campus and the city.

The Tripolia Gate (three-arched gate), the next pause en-route, is the major transition node denoting the onset of the royal realm and affords the first glimpse of the palace facade. It also frames the ensemble composed of lateral massing across the facade and elements protruding to form the interface with the external world.

This route now arrives at a large court called the Bada Chowk. It is a contained space with an extended volume due to the presence of the high palace wall, the Tripolia Gate, the palace and the *silahkhana*–the place for meetings, etc. The Tripolia Gate is visually aligned to a structure across the courtyard which houses a large statue of Lord Ganesha at a higher level, inviting the movement towards it and marking the auspicious beginning into the royal precinct. Bada Chowk, used for recreational purposes and during festivities, finds higher plinths and *jharokhas* extending from the palace to allow voluntary participation as a one-way communication from inside out.

The entry into the palace is pronounced through three visual codes: the first being the entrance as the only puncture in the

1

2

3

4

opaque stone wall offset from the otherwise plain facade on the ground floor; the second being the flight of steps protruding from the facade plane; while the third is the large royal emblem in brass placed over the entranceway. This forms the formal and the pedestrian entry.

Entry for insiders and royal members riding elephants, horses and camels is a little further down, the zone functioning as the pivot of the City Palace between the *zenana* and *mardana* zones.

The eastern expanse of the citadel, within the palace, falling to the right of the movement path, is suggested by the deflecting wall plane mounted by the image of Lord Ganesha, arresting further movement. It is further pronounced by the recessed mass of the gateway sucking one in. The arched gateway called Toran Pol is also adorned with the royal emblem. Blank walls with elephant and soldier motifs painted on them arrest the visual axis here. Both entries into the palace are from the east, further reinforcing allegiance to the Sun God.

The next arrival court is called Moti Chowk. It is surrounded by walls and is featured by a tree in the centre and a raised deck to the north. These platforms receive dignitaries directly from the elephant's back.

Two walls meeting at right angles essentially create this arrival space over an elevated platform. The corner junction is the entryway called Ganesha Deoli. The pedestrian entry from Bada Chowk also connects to this point. The entrance is pronounced further by near life-size paintings of an elephant and a horse on the two perpendicular walls. At an entry to the *mardana*, a statue of Ganesha in the niche *en-face* the entrance cutout marks the beginning of movement. This also creates a baffle wall and an indirect entry. This deflection exposes a stairway leading to the upper level, which houses the actual living spaces. The stairs end at a landing platform with opaque planes arresting the visual axis and highlighting the image of Bapa Rawal, the key person in the ancestral lineage.

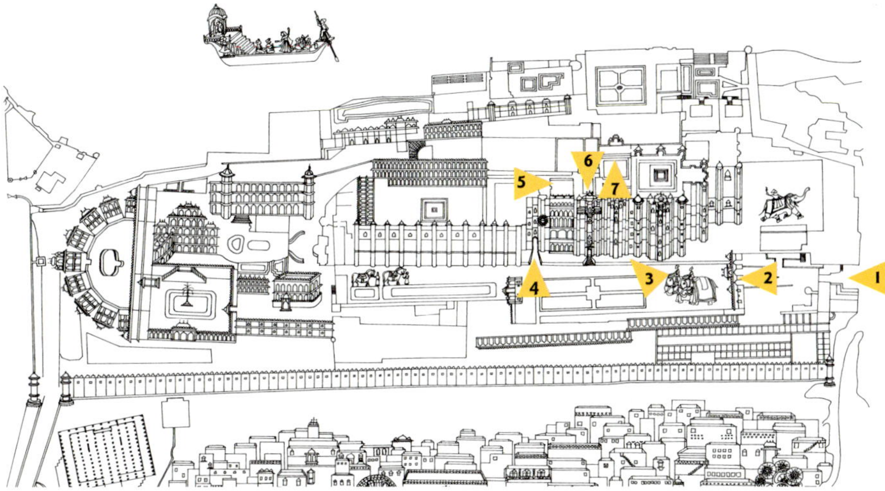

▲ City Palace showing the position of nodes.

◄5 6▼

7▼

1: Badi Pol leading to the Tripolia Gate.

2: Tripolia Gate providing a further threshold to Bada Chowk.

3: Formal pedestrian entry to palace marked by the projecting mass, royal emblem, extending steps and the entrance cutout.

4: Alternate entry to the palace through the recessed archway for the royal entourage.

5: Raised platform at the Moti Chowk to receive dignitaries and guests directly from the elephant's back.

6: Near life-size paintings of elephants and horses on the perpendicular wall with cornered incision to mark the entry which features an idol of Lord Ganesha in a niche.

7: Narrow stairway leads to the upper level, where light attracts the perceiver to the right.

One arrives at Rajyangan, the royal court, which is surrounded by living spaces on the east and west and walls along the north and south. The eastern zone is a royal arrival court while the western zone consists of a shrine of the deity Dhunimata, facing the east. The straight movement is stopped here and after a due pause, one is guided to the left where winding stairs lead to the Chandra Mahal with *jharokhas* overlooking the lower Rajyangan court.

This ensemble so far culminates as the highest and furthest end of the movement path during the initial phases of development. The water basin, a relief of a nymph and statues of women holding mirrors and other cosmetic components refer to the space as a personal one reserved only for the royal couple and the queens.

Being sited on a hill, the further spaces of the citadel are added at the upper levels, automatically changing the privacy levels and the hierarchy of spaces.

A flight of stairs connects the Chandra Mahal to the next space located at the highest level of the palace and which is called Badi Mahal or the Garden Palace. This consists of a large, open-to-sky courtyard with a garden and large trees in the middle. The vegetated court is surrounded by arcaded semi-covered verandah spaces on three sides and a living pavilion with its own water pond adorning the fourth northern side.

This would have been the court for family entertainment, festive celebrations and special meetings. The garden, pavilions, verandahs, water channels and the animated flooring patterns enhance the festive mood.

8: The stairway opens out into the Rajyangan court.

9: The next level above the Dhunimata shrine is Chandra Mahal where images of nymphs and water basins speak of intimate spaces.

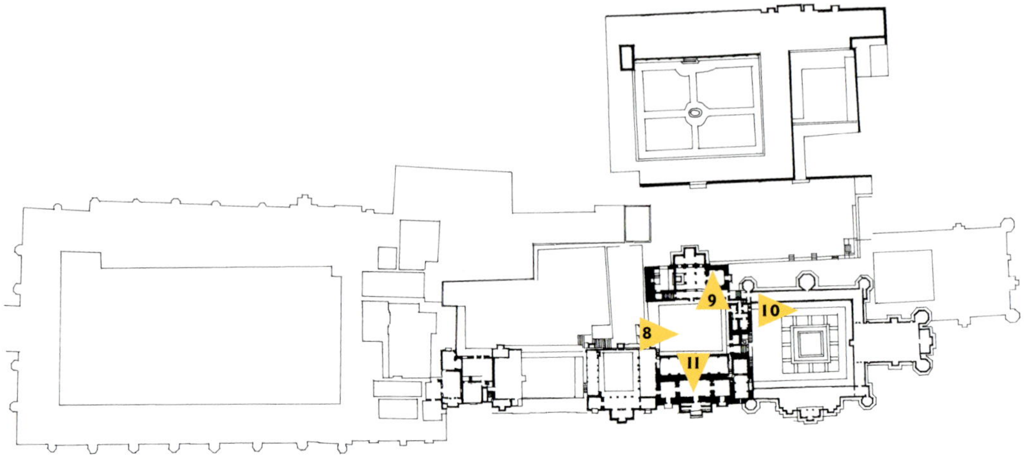

Fourth level of the City Palace showing the various nodes.

8

9

10

11

Opposed to the simplicity in forms and massing seen during the initial phases, the spaces developed during the later periods show tremendous refinement and intense adornment. Passing through the Dilkhush Mahal, Kanch ki Burj–spaces with elaborate glass and mirrorwork–and the Krishna Nivas, one reaches a terrace pavilion. Cladded with colorful mosaic on the walls as well as the domical ceilings, the rooms of Dilkhush Mahal are enchanting and exotic, especially due to the multiple reflections and glow of the lamps in the niches. The Krishna Nivas is alternatively adorned with wall paintings depicting various events and activities around the palace.

The other return routes interlinked with this peak of exotic pleasure are equally intertwined, circuitous and full of experiential variety. As spaces are organized around the courts and linked through narrow stairs and passages, they unfold gradually and sequentially through twists and turns. Each baffle invites one to pause, absorb and reorient. They also provide the much-needed transition, physical as well as mental, to experience the diverse spaces and varied ambiences.

The Badi ChatursHali is the outdoor terrace pavilion reached after these rooms. Walls surround it on three sides and a pavilion overlooking the city forms the fourth side.

The light filtering through the cutouts along the eastern face of this pavilion and the adornment of bright blue ceramic tiles draws the onlooker towards the perpendicular axis of the movement. The corresponding arched openings and *chhatri* pavilions on the opposite walls further emphasize this east-west axis. These arches frame views of Udaipur City towards the east and of the Lake Palace on the west.

10: The Badi Mahal with trees, fountains and embellished floors create a festive ambience outdoors.

11: The Dilkhush Mahal with stained glass openings and reflective mirror work provides for pomp and ceremony within.

Dutch and Chinese ceramic tiles cladding the columns, walls and ceilings radiate an aura of the Mediterranean and Europe. The depiction of Biblical stories (escape from Egypt) on the tiles within the framed niches or on the door panels further enhance this sense. Moti Mahal and Surya Prakash are the places next in succession to reach the Priyatam Nivas at the upper level and the Mayur Chowk at the lower.

Moti Mahal is, once again, an alluring space with a profusion of intricate mirror and stained-glass work. The light filtering through the stained glass, the reflections of the mirrors and polished floor, and the vibrancy of colours provide an enchanting ambience. This light filtering through the glass paintings and the stained glass windows acts as the next guiding element and a conditioning link to another richly decorated space, the Suraj Gokhra, which is inlayed with mother-of-pearl and semi-precious stones. This space also displays the royal emblem. Perhaps the seat for the royal throne, it also opens into the Mayur Chowk–an ornate courtyard with peacock murals in glass and mirrors depicting the three seasons. The Suraj Gokhra and the Manek Mahal position themselves at opposite ends of the Mayur Chowk.

The overwhelming presence of royal emblems, inlaid portraits of kings, statues of ancestors and various seals and insignia symbolizes the royal court and the place for dignitaries. This completes the circuit leading back to Moti Chowk, which is connected to the *zenana* on the other side.

Third level plan showing the various realms.

The corner position and the recessed location of the gate makes it automatically less inviting and presents a bottleneck as the entry into the women's court is restricted. Apart from the opacity of the wall (without fenestration) and the presence of tall gates, privacy is maintained through an indirect access. A baffle wall is once again placed in front–again with motifs of Lord Ganesha–to mark the beginning, a new entry sequence. Light from the adjoining court attracts movement towards it and this constricted space opens out into a large court known as the Laxmi Chowk surrounded by the queen's chambers. The large scale of courts and the presence of large trees, water fountains and gardens along with temples and pavilions constitute the 'outdoor' world to which the royal ladies would largely be confined. This becomes the most introverted realm.

Thus, the City Palace indeed presents numerous worlds within a world. Each layer unfolds to expose a new one and the journey through these thresholds continually conditions the mind. Spatial sequencing to abstract symbolism both play important roles in the interactive process of design communication and of offering subtle clues about the further progression of movement as well as the intended mood and nature of the space to come.

12

12: The Badi Chaturshali, a blue ceramic tile cladded pavilion overlooking Udaipur City.

13: Passage with stained glass windows filtering colorful light is a conditioning link to the formal royal spaces. Photo courtesy: Dilip Karpoor

14: The embellished wall and decorated *jharokha* overlooking Mayur Chowk.

15: Mayur Chowk, a formal royal court with grand and elaborate detailing.

16: Laxmi Chowk is surrounded by the queen's chambers and is a large introverted landscaped court with fountains and pavilions creating a leisurely environment.

13

14

15

16

As a royal campus, the City Palace has diverse functions and composite spaces to offer. Each space is intended to create its own ambience and induce an appropriate mood.

Notions of formal and casual, royalty and commoner, family and outsiders, the *mardana* and the *zenana*, official and leisurely are essentially conveyed through surface articulation, decor and association of semiotics.

Grandeur and formality is manifest at the royal courts (offices) such as Manek Mahal and Suraj Gokhra across the Mayur Chowk. The use of mother-of-pearl and precious stone inlay bespeaks their status and richness. The royal emblems, sculptures and profiles of kings along the stained glass panelled corridors become visual reminders of the royal status of the personage.

Stained glass compositions depicting diverse floral and geometric patterns, colours in glass work interacting with sunlight, peacock murals depicting the seasons in coloured glass and mirror work all contribute towards the creation of the ambience of the outdoors and nature.

The mirror mosaics and glass inlays are used consciously to add an attribute of flamboyance to the personal rooms through multiple reflection of images as well as light. The Manek Mahal and Kanch ki Burj are excellent examples of such illusory, hallucinating environments created for dancers, who charmed the king.

◄1 2

3

4 ►

The romantic aura is radiated in other private chambers such as the Chandra Mahal through elements such as the water basin, stone reliefs of nymphs and ladies holding *shringar* (elements of adornment), such as mirrors, *kum-kum* (red powder), and perfumes.

Painted motifs are also explicitly used at the Udaipur palace, especially the near life-size paintings of elephants and horses, which signify major gates and entry points for the riders. The prominent entrances to the major areas are also signified by the presence of idols of Lord Ganesha marking the beginning.

Thus, at the City Palace at Udaipur, the crafted and skillful overlay of motifs, symbols, artwork and colour in the decor further enhances the communication that the space enjoys with the exalted perceiver. The sheer choice of colours and the sensitive articulation of light to set this off into a million dazzling explosions in the space frees one from mundane day-to-day existence and makes one feel like a king, even if only for that brief time and space. The configuration of spaces and implied functions of these are expertly manoeuvered by the apt usage of conjured associations, notions about space, its ambience and the implied dictums.

1: Labyrinthine channels of the water fountain at the Laxmi Chowk exhibit strong formal geometry.

2: Glass and mirror mosaic mural at Mayur Chowk in the form of a peacock.

3: Stained glass windows for filtering light, and providing visual privacy.

4: Depiction of horse and elephant riders and soldiers marching along doorway to signify entry.

Following pages: Panoramic view of the imposing facade of the City Palace as seen from the lake.

SARKHEJ RAUZA
AHMEDABAD

View across from an overlooking balcony towards the queen's tomb.

Miniature style representation of the Sarkhej Rauza showing various domains.

The Context

On the southwestern fringe of Ahmedabad City lie the mosque, tomb and royal complex of Sarkhej. Popular as a retreat, the campus was initiated in 1446 by the Sultanate king Muhammad Shah, the son of Ahmed Shah, who founded Ahmedabad. The initial phase included the mosque and a tomb of Ahmed Khattu Ganj Baksh–a Sufi saint and one of the four legendary Ahmeds who laid the foundations of Ahmedabad City. The *khanqah* (resting place) of the saint, the Sarkhej complex was built in phases and was eventually completed over a decade later by the then king of Gujarat, Muhammad Begara, who added the large water tank with steps all around, along with the king and queen's pavilion as summer retreats. The tombs of the king himself, his wives and the immediate family have also been laid out in the same campus.

1: The tank with *ghat*-like steps leading into the water with the tombs and the mosque seen in the background.

2: Miniature style impression of the Sarkhej complex showing the extent of the tank and its relation to the mosque, tombs and the royal complexes.

1

2 ►

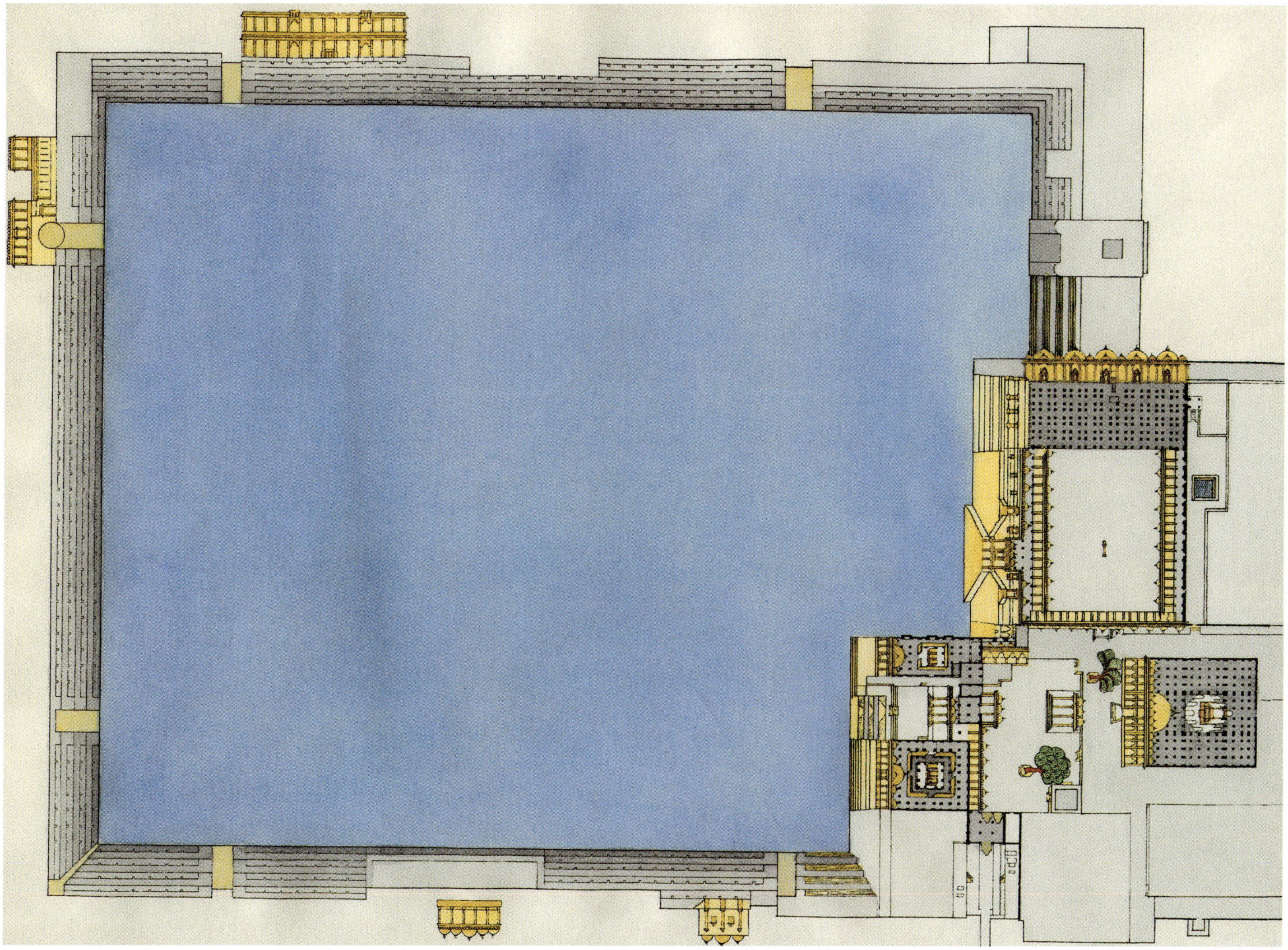

The Construct

The *rauza* (tomb) complex at Sarkhej built at the advent of the Sultanate era is an apt example of Indo-Saracenic architecture from this region where Hindu and Islamic influences are fused together. Hindu craftsmanship and construction know-how was overlaid upon the Islamic sense of geometry and scale. A trabeated structural system in sandstone with corbelled domes and non-structural arched panels as infill testify to its stylization by Hindu craftsmen while the reference to square geometry and a rectilinear structural grid, floral or geometric patterns in filigree are the consequence of the Islamic discipline of entablature. The fusion and the eventual spatial organization, however, remain very Indian.

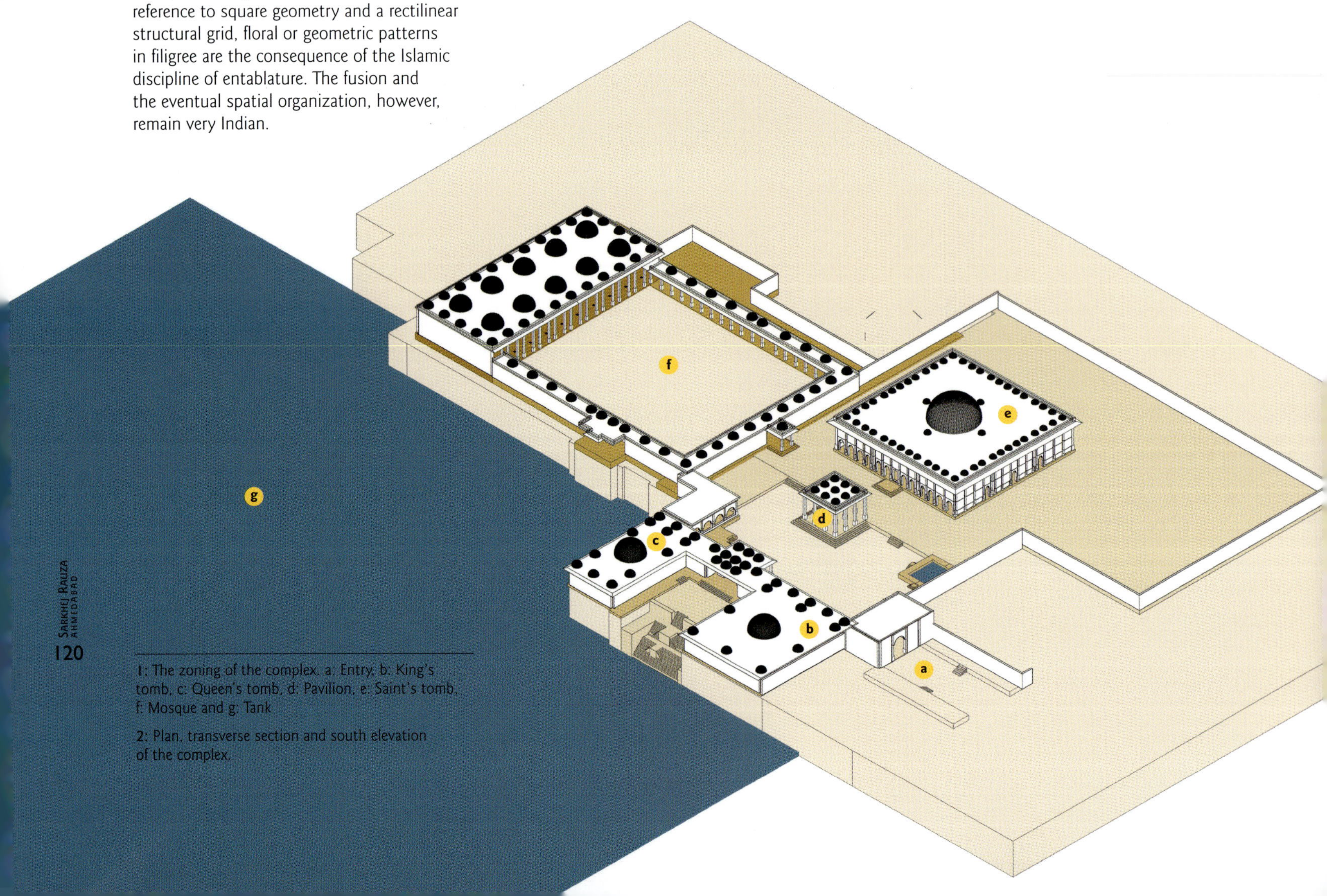

1: The zoning of the complex. a: Entry, b: King's tomb, c: Queen's tomb, d: Pavilion, e: Saint's tomb, f: Mosque and g: Tank

2: Plan, transverse section and south elevation of the complex.

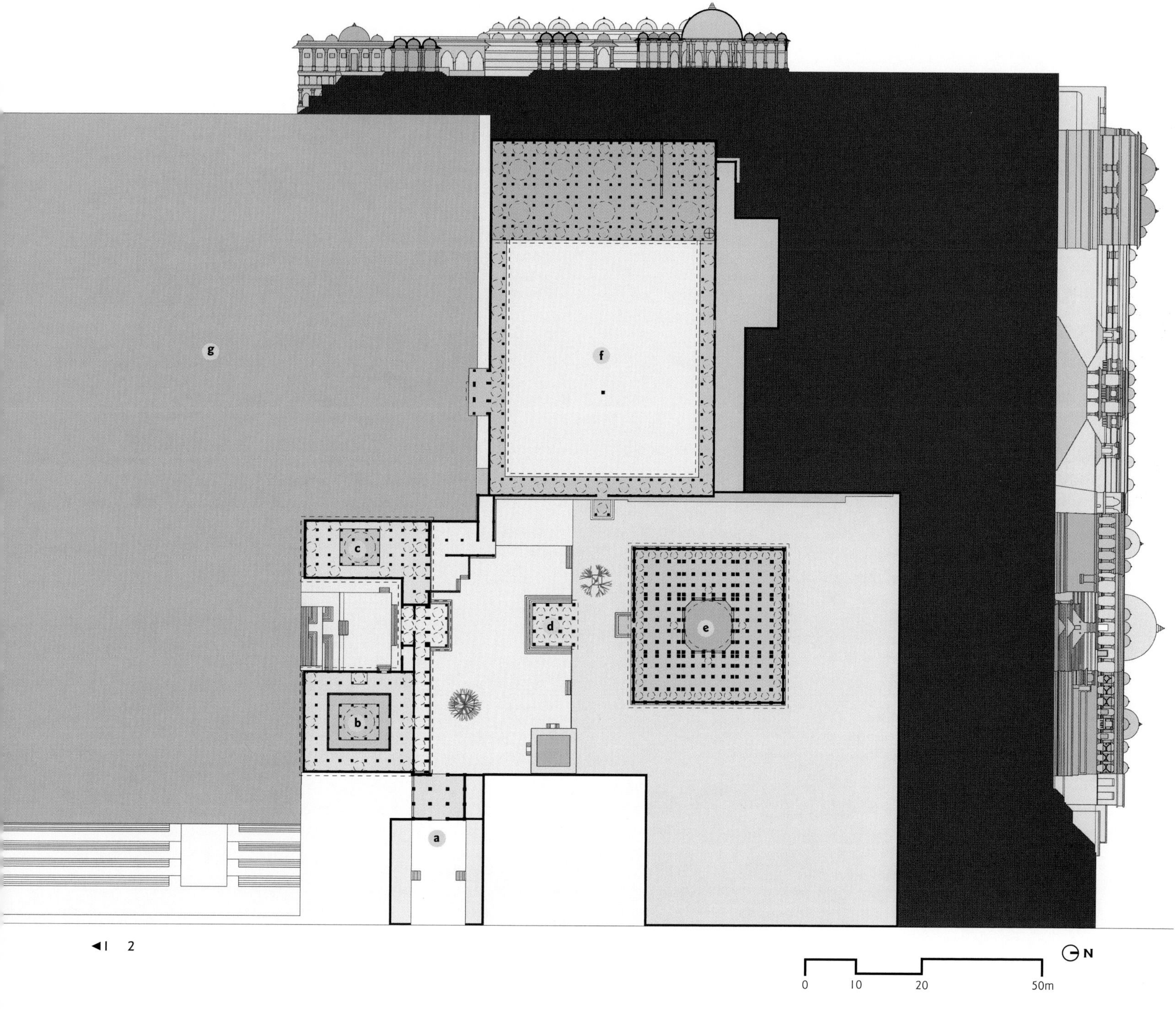

a
b
c
d
e
f
g
◄1 2
0
10
20
50m
N

The campus has three easily definable realms. The first one is the royal retreat consisting of a water tank and the king's and the queen's pavilions. The second comprises the tombs of the saint, the king and the queen, while the third is the religious one with a mosque and a cloistered fore-court. Three worlds coexist in this campus, each with its own focus, ambience and activities.

The first and the outermost world is the leisure node. Originally meant for royalty, it was subsequently transformed into a civic space. The rectilinear man-made water tank oriented north-south, is one of the key components of this realm. The tank is contained within and accessed through *ghat*-like stone steps and platforms on three sides while the mosque and tomb's walls form the fourth. This built edge on the north along with the summer pavilions for the king and queen along the southwestern corner of the tank give the void of the tank a sense of volume and containment. Conceived as a retreat, it exploits natural and environmental conditions for favourable effects and comfort conditions. The tank harvests natural rain-water from the region and offers pleasant views as well as soothingly cool breeze. The setting sun behind the queen's pavilion and the crescent of the moon in the canopy of the stars reflected in the still waters of the tank enhance its leisurely aura.

1: Water tank–the worldly realm.

2: Saint's tomb–the social realm.

3: The mosque–the sacred realm.

Defined by the royal tombs on the south, the saint's tomb on the north, the mosque's *riwaq* or arcaded verandah on the periphery and the entrance gateway on the east, the second court is a social world. Filled with people during festivals and on special prayer days, it becomes a platform for social interaction. Spontaneous commercial activities and the hustle-bustle of hawkers selling eatables, toys and seasonal goods personify the social milieu and the realities that make us a part of this world. The tombs of the royals also reinforce the ultimate reality that any mortal has to face. However, the saint's tomb with its large dome remains the dominating element and a soul-centre of this world. The priest is given a higher status as he is a link–the oracle and the guide–to God. And guide he does, indeed, through the positioning of his tomb.

The third realm, the most sacred world of the mosque, is reached further by the saint's tomb. This sacred world is the innermost and is defined by the mosque-space (*liwan*) in the west facing holy Mecca and the colonnaded *riwaq* on the other three sides, retaining a rectilinear courtyard (*sahak*) in the middle. This creates a fully withdrawn, highly concentrated, heavily insulated and most tranquil space of the campus, helping one to focus on the ultimate goal–God.

The mood, identity, as well as the sanctity of each world are, thus, maintained. Each world exists, in its entirety, on its own and yet at a different scale, each world remains a part of the larger whole and complements the other parts. For example, the projecting balconies, *jharokhas* and openings on the contiguous long wall along the tank, while holding the water's edge, create a streetscape as a familiar backdrop and reminder of the city's skyline with domes in silhouette. What appears to be a continuous facade from the water forms different parts from the inner edge and performs very different roles. For example, the wall is a perforated stone *jali* or screen at the king's tomb while as the *liwan* in the mosque, it becomes a solid wall. Similarly, the eastern wall of the mosque contains the void of the fore-court in the tomb quadrant. The single, largest dome over the saint's tomb, although eccentrically placed within the complex, remains the perceptual and notional centre, uniting the three worlds and serving as mutual reference. Thus, the schema of centre and sub-centre, the whole as a part and the part as a whole, is effectively personified in this campus. Courtyards and dual-edged built interfaces, becoming self-referential to different worlds within and without, achieve this at Sarkhej. This principle of organization has emerged as the most effective spatial tool allowing for flexibility of development with phased growth addition and alteration over time. Each phase continues to function as a complete entity while effectively fusing in with the next phase. It also helps maintain the identity of each sub-centre yet respecting the allegiance it holds to the whole.

◄1

2

3

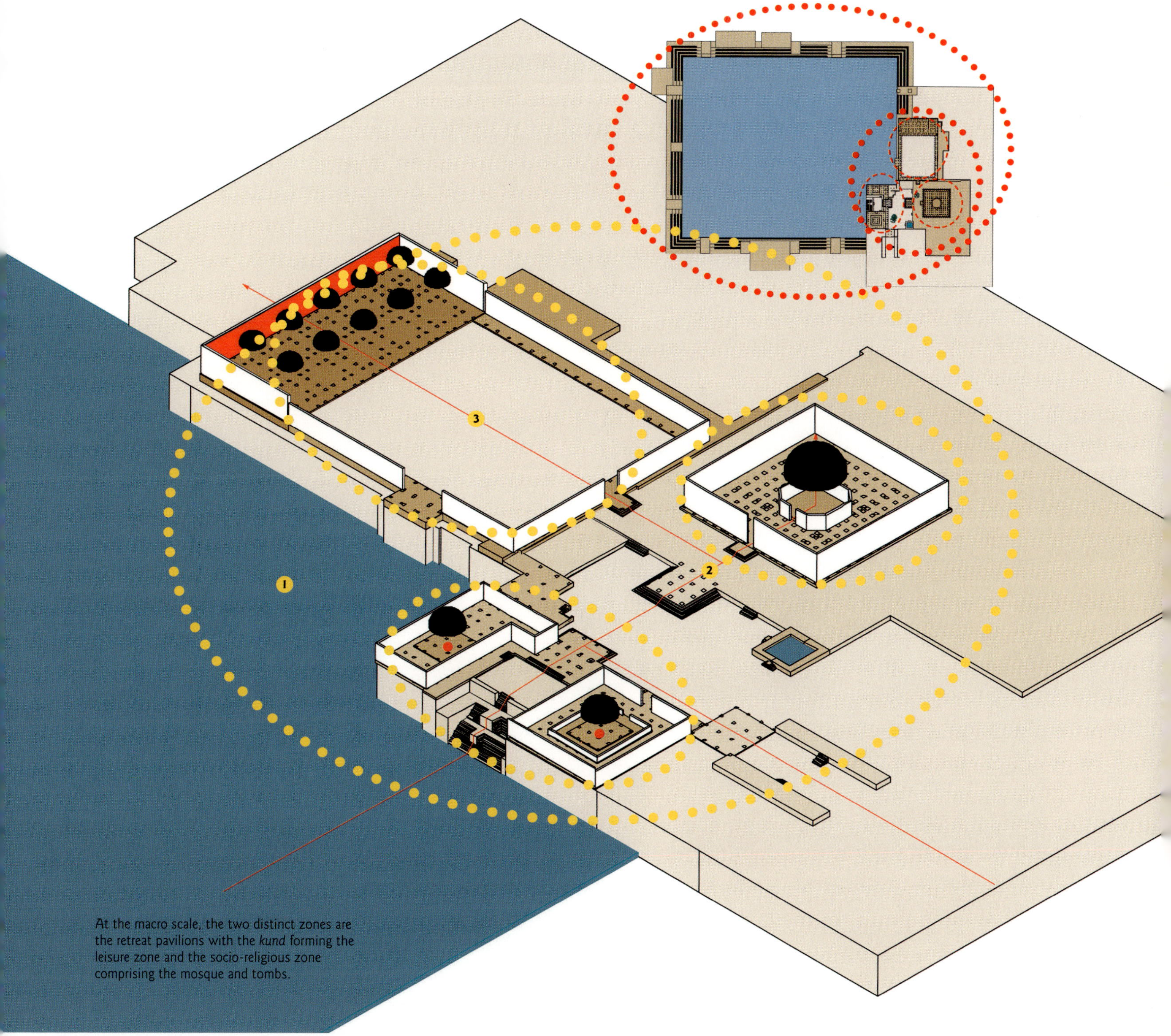

At the macro scale, the two distinct zones are the retreat pavilions with the *kund* forming the leisure zone and the socio-religious zone comprising the mosque and tombs.

Historian Clause Herdec in his treatise 'Formal Structures in Indian Architecture' presents a theory on the possible phases of the *rauza's* development over time. It hypothesizes the presence of a fountain along the east-west axis of the entrance gateway. The entire sequence of approach from here to the various parts of the complex is a process of visual, perceptual and conceptual communication. The effective usage of such non-axial compounded arrangements of spaces with separated realms, diverse user-groups and even more diversity of functions facilitates a creative communication process between the visitor and the space. At Sarkhej, this process is spontaneous, intuitive and personal as spatial encoding is subconsciously perceived and deciphered by the observer as he moves through space.

The first clue to the premise from what would have been the fountain node is the Islamic-arched gateway. A deep gateway marks the first threshold from the outer world. Not aligned axially to other parts of the campus, it invites one to explore. From here, on being sucked towards the colonnaded edge of the king's tomb, the cooler, dark space beckons one from the scorching heat outside automatically and the visual cone directly registers the entry to the king's tomb.

1. The arched gateway as the first transition structure into the complex.

2: The colonnade, arrested by the protruding pavilion, defines a suction space, a node and a clue for movement towards the royal tomb.

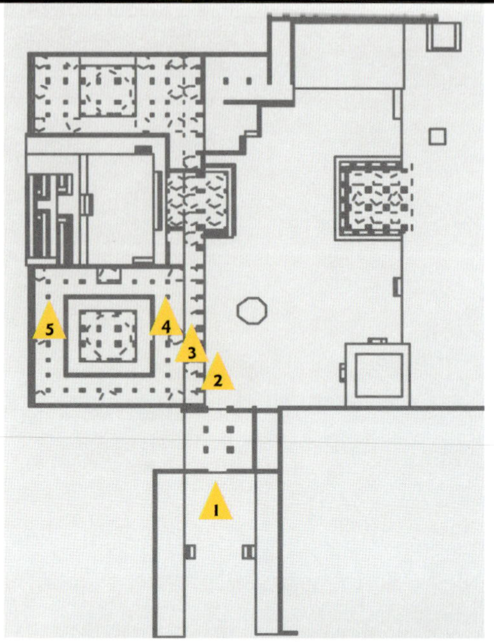

Plan showing the position of nodes.

1

2

3

4

5

As one enters the precinct, the secondary layers of spaces as the peripheral movement bay and the square inner core contained by the column grid, the raised plinth and the volume under the dome are revealed. The tomb, placed under the dome in the inner core, falls on the axis from the entry bay, and the intensity of light is low. As against this, the light penetrating through the peripheral stone screen walls is stronger and as a result it draws one to walk around the tomb in an anti-clockwise manner. After the conditioning of the eye and mind from the harshness of light through the playful shadow patterns of the lattice walls, one arrives at the central core of the tomb.

3: Colonnade provides transition from the outdoors, inviting entry into the royal tombs.

4: Circumambulatory around the tomb although symmetrically arranged, invites movement towards the right (west) due to the screen walls and kinetic shadow patterns with penetrating light.

5: Screens admit mellow light into the space, cool breeze from the tank and privacy from outside.

On emerging from the king's tomb one faces the saint's tomb. It becomes the next reference. The saint's tomb also consists of a peripheral bay, *jali* walls and an inner core, with an octagonal chamber surmounted with a dome. Although larger in size, the spatial impact, physical elements and the conditioning rituals remain similar to the king's tomb.

Exiting the saint's tomb, one is attracted to and deflected by the free-standing pavilion structure consisting of a square plinth space, columns and dome. This pavilion becomes a pivot in the centre of the whole organization–a built mass in the midst of an unbuilt void of open space. Further attracted by the tree with the raised plinth and the projecting entry mass on the west, one is drawn towards the mosque.

Through the court (*sahak*) or the colonnaded *riwaq* along the periphery, one could reach the *liwan*, *en-face* the *mehrab*–the niche in the *quibla* wall facing Mecca. The blank wall edging along the outer face of the *riwaq* empirically creates a very contained, concentrated space helping further to create a focus and emphasizing the west-facing *quibla* wall. However, on the southern face there is a deviation by way of *jharokhas* looking out into the tank and pavilions further away.

7

6

8

9

10

11

12

13

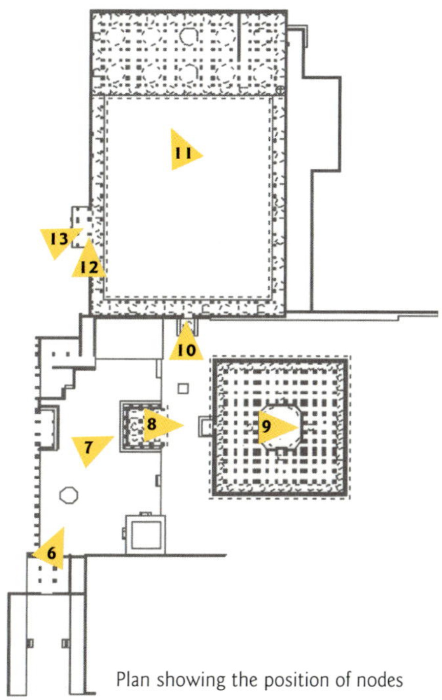

Plan showing the position of nodes

6. Protruding pavilion *en-face* entrance archway provides a clue for an alternate movement route to the water as well as to the mosque.

7. Free-standing, colonnaded pavilion as pivot relays further movement towards the saint's tomb.

8. Framed view of the saint's tomb from the colonnaded pavilion.

9. Saint's tomb, a structure within a skin.

10. Cutout within a blank wall and projecting portico guiding movement towards the mosque.

11. Movement pulled towards the left through projecting balcony and openings towards the tank.

12. The *riwaq*, an arcade enclosing the mosque court (*sahak*).

13. View towards the lake framed by the balcony.

Stepping out of the mosque, one is again confronted by the open pavilion. Acting as a pivot it provides a pause and orients one to other references. One obvious reference falling on the axis of the pavilion towards the south is the projecting porch and plinth mass leading to the water tank. The descending steps along the axis and intermediate platforms with tapering degree of wall enclosure provide a gradual transition from the contained to the open, from the within to the without. The cascading platforms finally dissolve into *ghat*-like steps before interacting with the water and hold the water's edge in harmony with the steps all around the tank. The king's and queen's pavilions–built outcrops in a barren skyline–naturally emerge as visual clues and form mutual references to each other from either side of the tank.

14: Free-standing pavilion aligned axially to the portico leading to the water-body.

15 and 16: Passing through the pavilion and into the portico framing views of the tank.

17: A court becomes the transition platform overlooking the water and contained by the prominent masses of the royal tombs.

18: Active interface with the water through steps.

Plan showing the position of nodes.

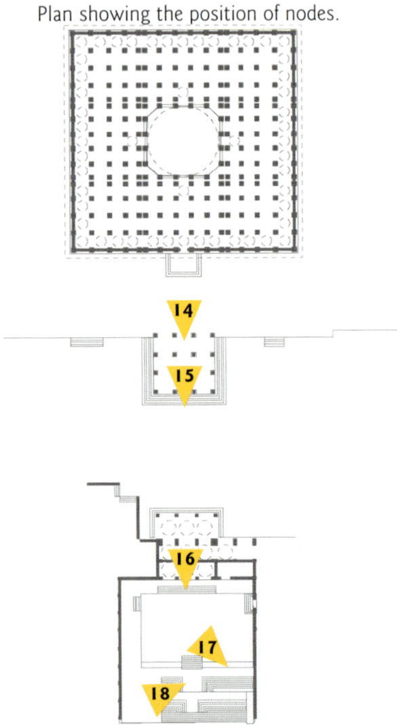

14

15

16

17

18

19

20

In response to the multiplicity of functions and their varied preferences among the users, there exist multiple choices of approaches and diverse sequence combinations at the Sarkhej complex. The first court surrounded by mausoleums, more specifically the pavilion and porches encroaching into the court, become the key nodes and pivotal in this respect.

For example, from the entranceway, the projecting porch of the southern edge can become the spatial clue for the approach to the water tank. The central pavilion becomes a critical reference element leading from the entranceway to the saint's tomb, alternatively framing and further leading to the tank from the mosque or the saint's tomb. It is also pivotal in directing one towards the mosque.

Similarly, the porch projecting from the *riwaq* wall in the east helps emphasize the entry point and so does the southern one for the water tank. The plinth and the tree play a vital role in directing movement towards the mosque entry by their axial positioning and as a counter element to the pavilion.

Sunlight has been incorporated into the system as a critical spatial element, which guides most directions through its intensity and shadow patterns such as in the *jalis*–perforated walls around the tombs. It also makes the spaces within cheerful and dynamic with the changing positions of the sun in the sky and the associated shadow patterns.

Thus, it is neither plan geometry, the cardinal points, nor the conditioned axial references but rather, the more intuitive and visual references that become the organizational tool at the Sarkhej complex. This in turn translates the perceptional sequence into an experience and the process of encoding-decoding, a subconscious event.

19: Spatial elements such as the projecting portico, free-standing pavilion, arched gate-way, and framed portals guiding movement at the Sarkhej complex.

20: View from the tank towards the tombs.

As a sacred structure of the Islamic faith, the Sarkhej campus observes the tenets of the religion and these notions are reflected in the principles of its architecture. The strongest of these, reflected here, is the aspect of geometry and symmetry. Individual structures are governed by the rotation of the square plan form and are symmetrical along their own central axis. As any depiction of live creatures is forbidden in Islam, the filigree is essentially in the form of square *jalis* carved in floral or geometric patterns. In the mosque, surrounded by the *riwaq* on three sides, the pull is achieved on the fourth side by the thickened wall mass of the *liwan*, the pronounced domes over them and particularly the small niche recess of the *mehrab*, both physically and associationally as the axis to God pointing towards the *quibla*.

One of the most dynamic compositions loaded with symbolism is the enlarged dome above the saint's tomb. This acts as a visual and notional fulcrum of the mosque and tomb campus. A reference point, suggestive of the teacher's position, held in high esteem, as the link between man and God. As a guide who leads one to the path of God, the saint's tomb, apart from its plinth elevation or the dome pronouncement, is also strategically placed as a pivot in-between the corporeal and the spiritual realm. The path to the mosque is also directed and revealed through it.

1: Stone grill as screen to filter light and afford privacy within. The geometric patterns are in keeping with the Islamic faith.

2: A miniature style expression where the saint's tomb becomes the centre from which emanates the energies radiating into all the other parts of the complex.

Pages 132-133: Leisure pavilions in silhouette at Sarkhej with the tank in the foreground.

1

2 ►

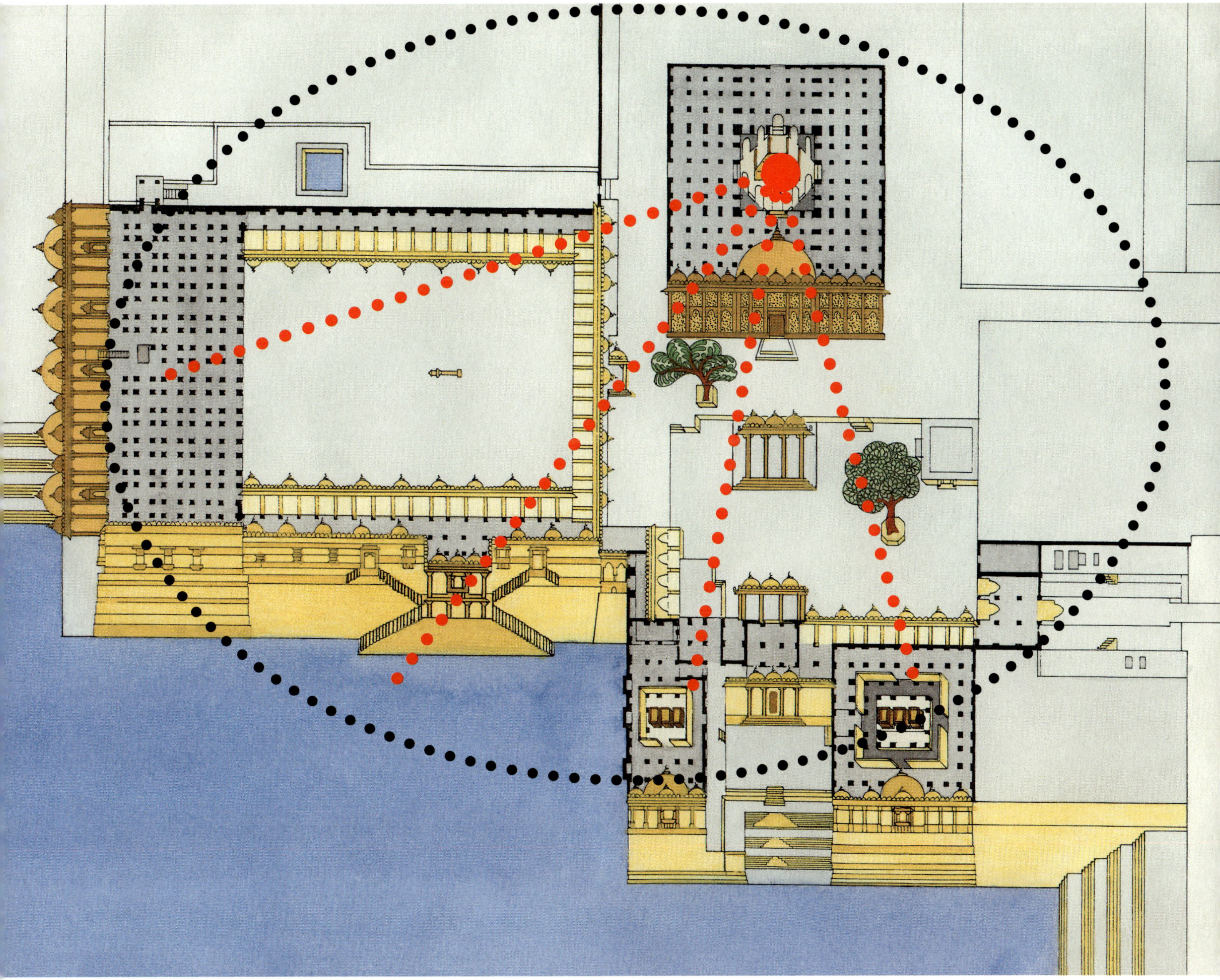

INFERENCE

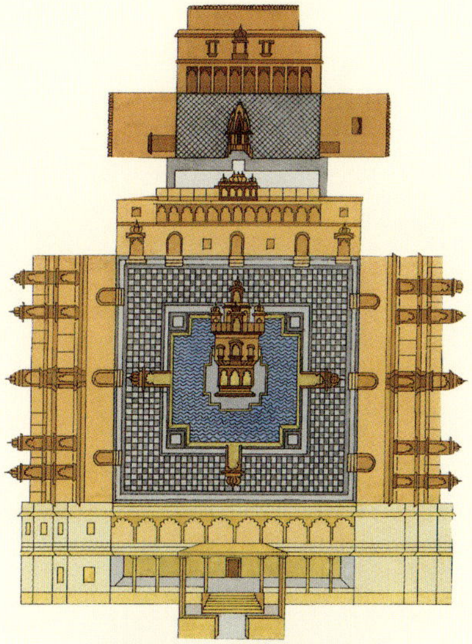

Understanding Historic Architecture through Spatial Perception

There are numerous approaches to reviewing historic architecture. The approach adopted by historians has been to try and understand the context of which the product has been an outcome. This helps in situating the product in its milieu and understanding the pressures of the given time and space. However, this approach falls short in establishing its position beyond the given time and space. Neither does it evolve principles or processes, which can be replicated in different contexts.

Archaeologists tend to look at these products as an ensemble of elements and sub-components. The stylization of these compositions and their typification becomes the essential datum of their study. This approach also remains stagnant and appropriate only to the given context. The understanding is valid for replication in terms of exact duplication rather than its interpreted transformation or appropriated adaptation to different conditions.

The concern of anthropologists lies chiefly in the exploration of the social messages encoded through symbols and metaphors as well as the correlation between the built and the social realm. This is a useful facet but only a part of the total experience. It involves a familiarity with, and conditioning by, the local context.

How then should an architect review historic architecture? Buildings outlast humans. Therefore, it becomes imperative that architecture transcends the given time-space context, remaining vital and adaptable to the changed ones. This refers to the universal qualities of builtform. Historic architecture has well established its universality and timelessness by remaining valid and vital over centuries.

Hence, as a space designer, what is of relevance to an architect is to learn from such historic architecture the generic principles of space organization that render them timeless. Correlation between spatial attributes and human behaviour, induced largely through perception of the space construct, helps the space designer interpret, extrapolate and apply the principles of space organization in a changed time and space, rather than replicate form, context, material, technology, styles and 'isms' which are ossified in history.

Technology advances with time. Seen in isolation, materials undergo transformation and change meaning with changed technological processes and are, thereby, largely a function of technology. Stylization loses relevance with the changed functional, technological or socio-political context. Symbols remain significant only within specific associations. Thus, what remains eternal and universal is the total spatial experience. Despite functional obsolescence, unknown historic background, irrelevant stylization and rudimentary technology, the fact that the spatial construct communicates through as a sensory perception, remains relevant for personal evaluation and experience. Such buildings emote purely at a human plane, making unnecessary any cultural conditioning or prior knowledge of the context.

Geometric coordination versus kinesthetics as a design tool

Numerous attempts have been made at analysing the spatial qualities through the structure of exemplary historic buildings to decipher and understand the generic ordering principles which make them unique. Most of these attempts have been diagrammatic, largely through geometric translations of the structural overlay in the form of orthographic drawings such as plans, elevations and sections. While these two-dimensional abstractions may be the tools of construction, they are not complete tools to evolve and communicate the development visions of the creators. They prove inadequate as well as inappropriate for simulating space perception and experience.

Plans, elevations and sections have an illusory point of view, which do not exist for the perceiver. The perceiver's cone of vision is very different from these orthographics and is also not static, since he constantly moves through the space. These diagrams fail to record such sensory aspects and therefore are reduced to geometric manipulations at an illusory plane. Geometric analysis of such diagrams leads to further distortion in comprehension. A dynamic tool, therefore, for conceiving and communicating the ideas related to spatial perception becomes essential.

Kinesthetics–perception in relation to movement–is a phenomenon inherent to any space-making. Only methods incorporating kinesthetics into the construct of space can integrate the human being and the three-dimensional matrix of space as an alchemy over time. The visual perception at the human eye-level while moving through the space provides the only accurate reality of spatial experience. Spaces designed keeping in mind this aspect of visual perception and the phenomenon of perception while in motion are experience-based and therefore effective. This is universal, predictable and sure to impact due to the consistency of the human scale, the eye-level and visual cone.

The distinction between geometric coordination and perspectival perception must be well understood. For example, the geometric centre of a square courtyard would remain the same whether the courtyard is four metres wide or fourteen. Thus, the plan diagram, geometrically coordinated, makes no difference in the relative placement of the centre. However, in reality, the centre being two metres or seven metres away from the perceiver makes a drastic difference in the visual cone and thereby the resulting space perception. This sensorial communication makes geometric coordination diagrams irrelevant. Similarly, the elevation diagrams show a visual composition without perspectival distortions, which should reveal additional facets implying depth, for a given point of view.

In plan when one mentions a reference, its meaning changes with the distance of the perceiver.

Positions A and B giving different vignettes.

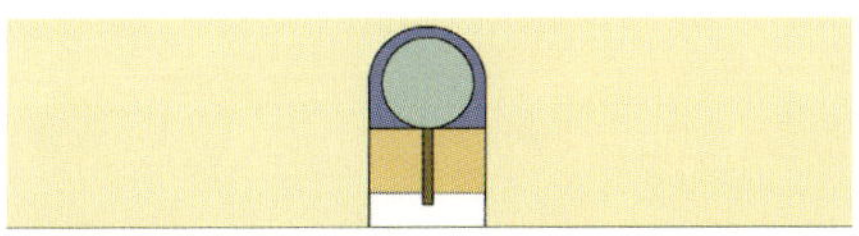

View from B

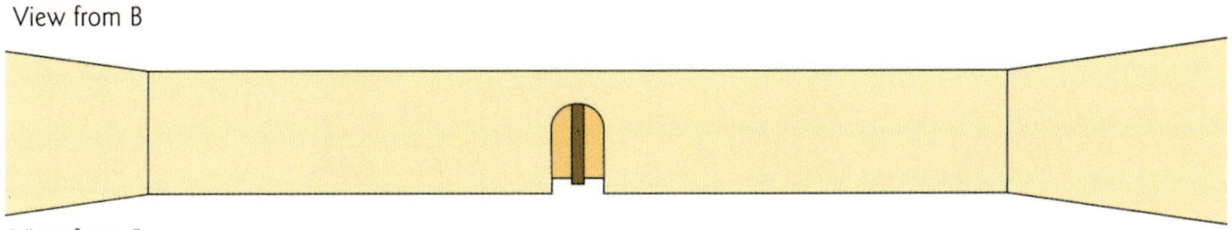

View from A

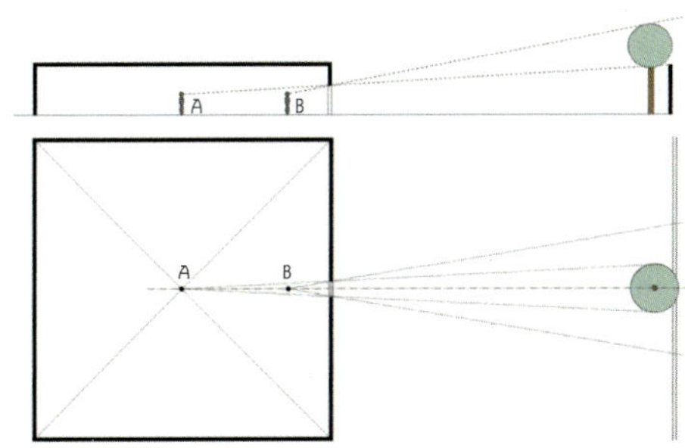

These principles due to their universality and timelessness have manifested themselves in various ways through time and have proved successful. Artists have best exploited the illusion of depth in otherwise two-dimensional drawings. Three-dimensional narratives were effectively encoded in two-dimensional miniature paintings of the 15th century in India. These chose to be representative of a time, mood and ambience rather than perspectively correct. There were many ways by which the artists effected communication and achieved emphasis in their creations. The content of the drawing was communicated as a narrative by manipulation of the overall composition so as to lead the eye sequentially from the important to the subtle. The visual weight and hierarchy was manipulated either by the central placement of important objects in a composition, exaggeration of their sizes or the uniqueness of the profile of the object under review. The overlay of plan with elevations, flipping of side views and the inclusion of foreground and background details, even though perspectively inaccurate, provided for the ambience and information on the general context. The holistic impression, thus created through the added layers of some immeasurable dimension, came closer to the desired experience of the depicted subject, through the interactive process of communication, actively involving the observer in it and allowing for intuitive perception.

1

2

3

1: Early 19th century Kangra painting depicting Queen Mena, the wife of King Himachal and mother of Parvati, awakening from her long sleep, as Yog-nidra, the goddess of yogic sleep leaves the Queen's body. Source: Shivpuran Portfolio, courtesy: Government Museum and Art Gallery, Chandigarh.

2: Late 19th century *pata* (cloth painting) depicting the *haveli* of Shrinathji at Nathdwara. Source courtesy: Amit Ambalal.

3: Eighteenth century *pichhwai* (wall hanging) depicting Annakuta, the offerings to Lord Shrinathji. Source courtesy: Amit Ambalal.

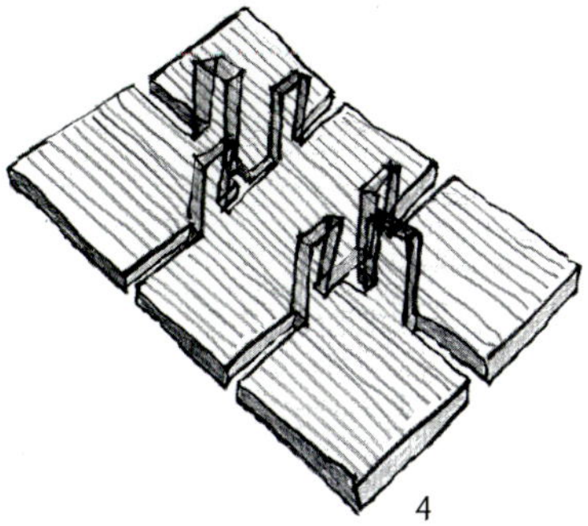

4

5

Inside-Outside:
Dissolution of boundaries

The phenomenon of visual and perspectival perception has also been well exploited by modern installation artists to create illusory and exciting frames. One such artist, who created installations on the principles of dynamic perception of visual frames, has been Krijn De Koning from the Netherlands.

According to his perception, "Reflection and history play a significant role in the way we look. But our lives are terribly influenced by concepts and ideas, and these sometimes get in the way a lot. That is perhaps why I find the physical mode of looking so intriguing. It gives you insight into a reality at that particular moment. In my work I often strip a space of its function, of its nature, in order to allow it to create its own reality. You allow it to be seen in a different light. How people look at things, while looking, and the way we remember that is the very essence of my work."

Though small in extent, its labrynthine nature and the effective use of colours create wonderful juxtapositions of the masses perceived and the voids carved out. These compositions are ever-changing in motion and, thus, the space becomes interactive, responsive and dynamic.

6

7

8

4-10: Different views of an installation at Central Museum, Utrecht, from various points, giving changed frames, references and perceptions depending upon the position.
Photos courtesy: Krijn De Koning

9

10

‘Promenade Architecturale’

The aspect of visual and perspectival narratives has been extrapolated into the realm of architecture and space design by the internationally renowned architect Le Corbusier. He has been known for his views on the ‘Promenade Architecturale.’ His architectural resolutions achieve spatial dynamics through creative juxtapositions of the visual and movement axis. The Ahmedabad Textile Mill Owners Association building at Ahmedabad is one of the most evolved explorations of the phenomenon.

At the Mill Owners Association Building, the first perceptible architectural gesture is the protruding ramp. It draws the visitor through and, since a walk over an inclined plane is a simultaneous displacement in the vertical and horizontal axes, it renders the first floor imperceptible as the elevated ground. The hand rail mass on the right edge of the ramp, the eccentrically placed continuous groove in the *kota* stone flooring, the ascending floor plane of the ramp–all converge in perspective onto the small backlit window aperture placed *en-face* in the baffle wall.

The triple height volume, like an entrance portal through the facade, offers a sense of arrival. Small openings through the baffle wall as well as the brightness of light penetrating through the eastern facade beyond, guides the route of the visitor further to the right edge. This junction then reveals the choice of other movement routes; one being towards the conference hall and administration, directed by the brightly painted and curved plane of the free-standing mass of the toilet; the other route is defined by the external stair mass leading to the next floor.

1

2

3

4

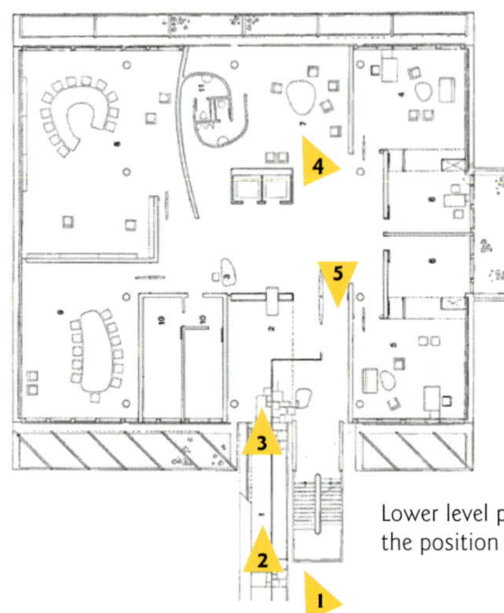

Lower level plan showing the position of nodes.

5

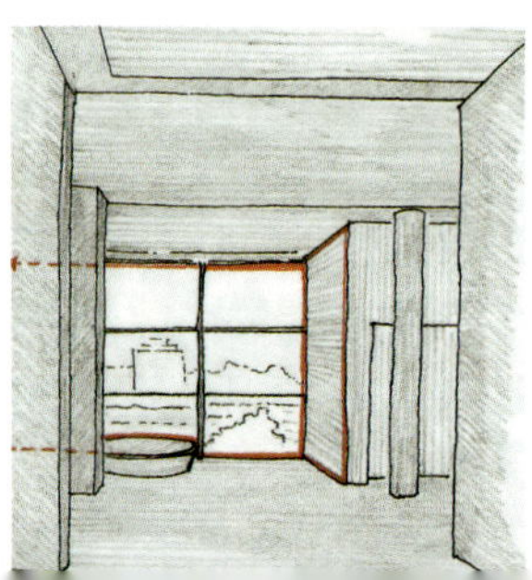

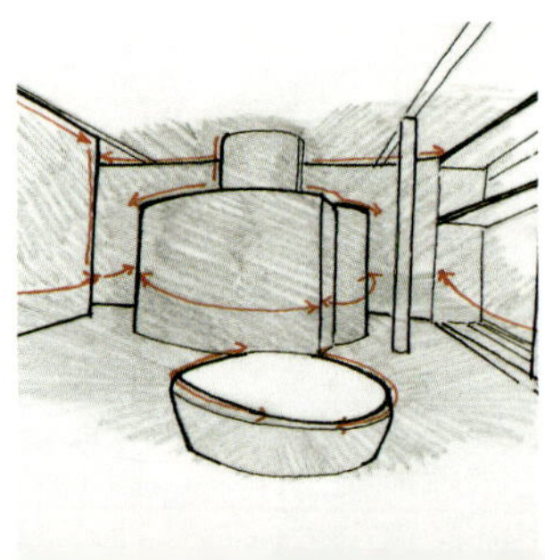

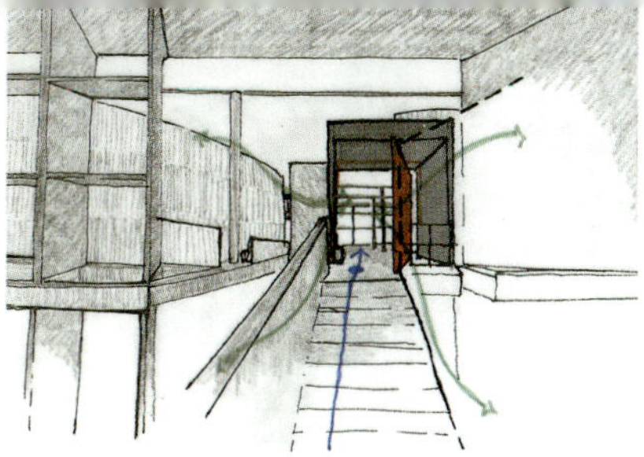

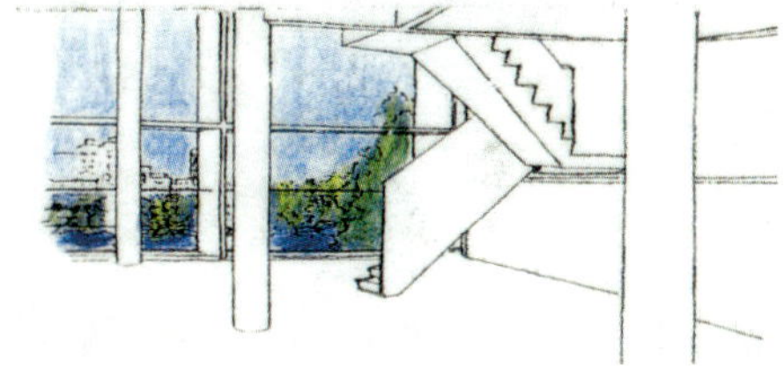

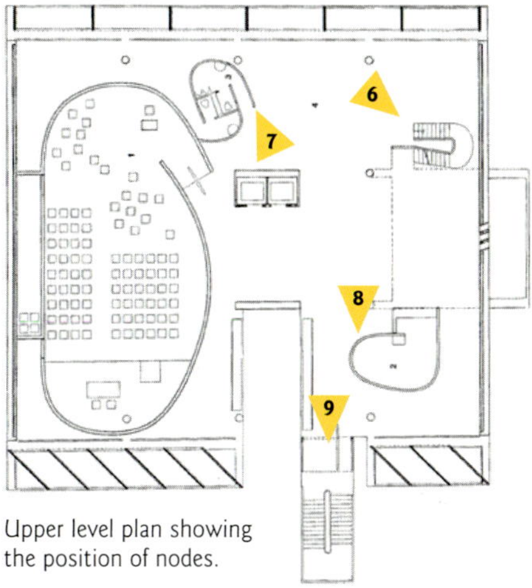

Upper level plan showing the position of nodes.

6

The eastern facade with perpendicular fins and horizontal concrete ties provides visual portals framing expansive vignettes across the river. While climbing by means of the external stairs, the high parapet taller than eye level takes away any outward distractions and maintains the introverted nature of the stairway and movement path.

The first floor once again offers more choices. The eccentric perception of the arrival portal at the staircase landing as one climbs up creates a visual axis diagonally towards the doorway. This, along with the involution of the curved wall plane, places an emphasis on the library space. The tapering curvatures of the elliptical walls and the deflected light off the inverted catenary shell ceiling helps focus attention on the stage within the library/lecture space.

The overlapping juxtapositions of frames through numerous perspectival alignments according to the movement, the closing and opening of light crevices created due to separated facade frames on the eastern and western sides and the inclined louver fins–the *brise-soleil*–on the west, further add to this visual drama due to the changing sense of apertures on the various wall planes along the path of movement.

Be it the visual alignment of elements; relative visual perception of free-standing mass as objects in space and guiding/scaling planes; the overlay of voids to conceal as well as reveal masses; the varying intensity of light to offer desired visual weight; the curving of wall planes as well as the use of colour to suggest movement direction are all the architectural nuances influencing spatial perception and manipulating its comprehension all along the movement. This renders the resolution dynamic, ever-changing, interactive and thereby timeless.

7

8

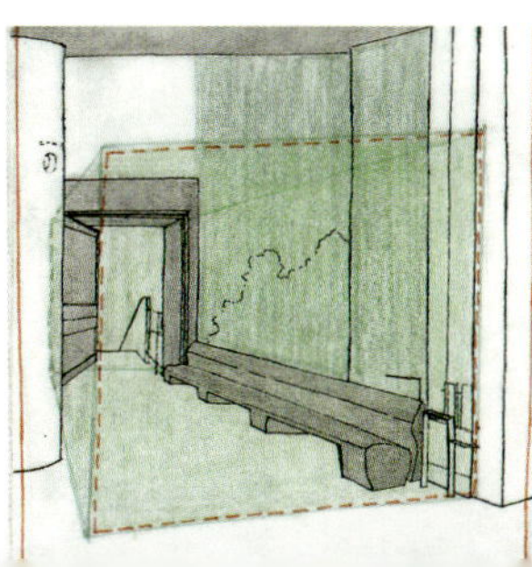

9

1, 2, 3, 4 and 5: Vignettes framed during motion from the entry to the upper level.

6, 7, 8 and 9: Vignettes framed during motion within the upper levels.

Sequential Unfolding of Spaces

A schema for Indian architecture

Traditional Indian architecture is essentially experiential, where predetermined vignettes are sequentially unfolded as one moves through the space. This simultaneous process of concealment and revelation of information brings about an element of mystery, inviting exploration. This sense of discovering space is orchestrated by the shift in the visual and physical axis. The introduction of physical buffers and the layering of spaces allow for each of these realms to function by themselves and yet creatively fuse into each another. Together they form the total structure. Penetration of each layer is rewarded by the further unfolding of an additional facet, offering yet another point of view or providing an additional detail. Such architecture, therefore, has to be discovered and perceived sequentially. Movement through the space is most critical rather than the externalities of form or the shape of elements. What matters here is the composite resolution of the ensemble and its multifarious frames from changing points of view–a time-space continuum.

This phenomenon of kinesthetics, thus, makes architecture experiential where 'being there' is what matters. These aspects of space organization remain universally perceptible yet retain specificity to the perceiver's own pace and mental constitution. This makes the experience profound through its plurality–the ability to respond to multiple value systems–and identity, the internalization of the experience by the perceiver.

Miniature style depiction of the studio, Sangath, highlighting the movement paths.

En route

The realms in-between

Indian architect Balkrishna Doshi's studio, Sangath, is an attempt to reinterpret Indian architectural traditions and find their resolution in a contemporary idiom. At Sangath, the dictums of spatial narratives in traditional architecture have been reinstated, making the architecture experiential.

The sequential unfolding of spaces, a gradual transition from the outdoors to the indoors and integration of the landscape are the principles of space-making here. Narratives are built into the organization, revealing themselves in an interactive manner.

Entrance to the premises is marked by an arrival court surrounded by a walled enclosure with a peephole glance beyond, through a window cutout, offering the visual clue of a design studio and activity beyond. The two-dimensional profile of the semi-circular vault is registered. However, the walls on three sides make one turn left. A gap in the low wall, flanked by an earthen pot on either side, further defines the path. The realigned axis helps one notice the undulating landscape and the metal sculpture placed to face the movement route, which otherwise may have remained unnoticed in the corner of the premises. A tree in the middle of the movement path makes one ponder and pause at the concave plinth profile. Pebble work of paving in the motif of a tree–a reminder of the once-existing mango tree at the spot–provides a node, offering vignettes of the vault. From a two-dimensional profile, the vaults now assume mass and appear solid.

The campus now assumes depth. The raised plinth maintains the visual reference of the building while consciously guiding the visitor further by means of a low wall.

A water-body dug into the ground is now revealed. The nearly diagonal corner of the site now affords a total panoramic view of the building with the complete stretch of the vault now appearing horizontally on the ground plane as well as vertically, through its reflection in the water. The water body also connects, visually as well as notionally, to the water harvesting gargoyle from the vaulted roof channel and the cascade of sequentially overflowing tanks and channels. Gradually ascending steps following the contours extend further to merge with the vaulted roof and disappear into the sky. The experience of a total outdoor landscape is then channelized further through a tapered side wall of the building gradually rising from the ground.

1

2

3

4

5

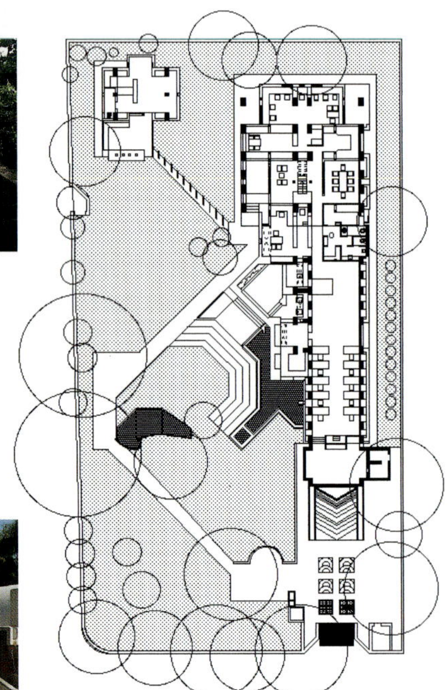

Plan of the studio

1: Oasis-like garden envelops the campus.
Photo courtesy: Rajeev Kathpalia

2: Paving guides vision towards punctured baffle wall.

3: Small opening within foliage reveals pathway with sculpture.

4: Water pond reveals the entire panorama.
Photo courtesy: John Panikar

5: Structure gains prominence with ambiguity in movement paths.

6

7

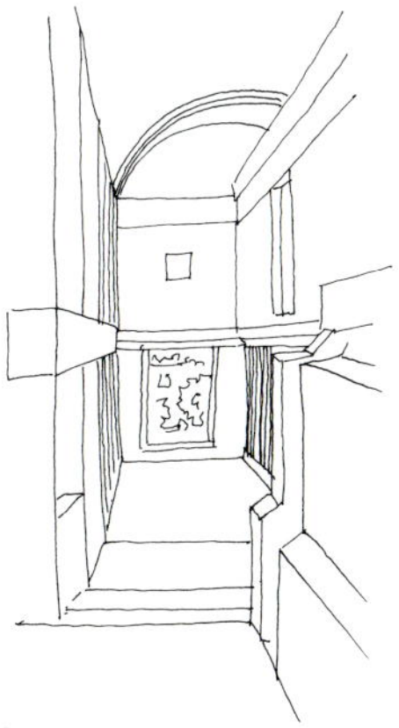

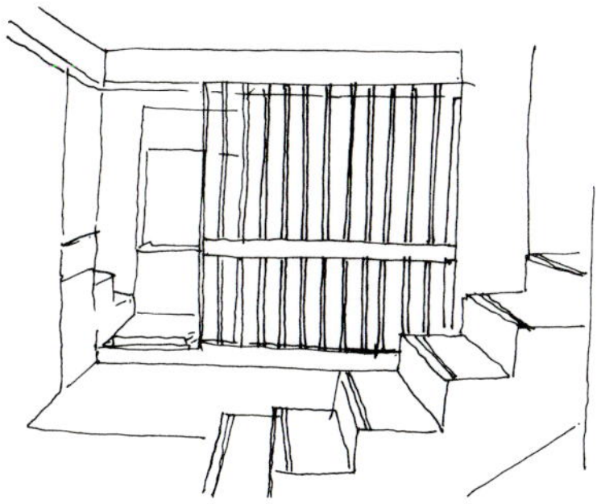

8

9

The large outdoors now gets a spatial definition through a side wall, which provides transition to a subsequent arrival space defined by the triple height volume of a vaulted roof and pilasters on the side. The near open arrival space with a high parasol extends further into the low volume enclosed space which visually and spatially extends beyond. It connects to the outside through a vertical louvred opening while extending within through the overlapping volume of the staircase and the mezzanine floor. Received in such a foyer space, the node further orients one to the studio through the visual link maintained along the axis of the vault, which accommodates the design studio, partly buried under the ground and disciplined by the elongated sequential space. The rear window now reconnects the studio back to the first arrival space near the entrance. Thus, from the arrival, the immediately adjacent space is actually approached last in the spatial sequence with a total 360 degree movement loop. Here, each turn, each pause, each node unfolds newer nuances for experiential enrichment and visual impact. Spatial narratives, by way of changing visual frames, overlaid symbols of paving patterns and the sense of transition through a varying combination of spatial elements successfully make the journey an event–an experience to personally relate to and explore.

Thus, the kinesthetics at Sangath demonstrates the holistic experience of architecture–an essential transformation of the past, for its relevance to the present and implied potential for the future.

6: The guiding plane of the wall mass moving the eye towards the double height.

7: The double height volume arresting movement towards it and exposing the narrow entry into the builtform.

8: The linear studio opening up once again to the small aperture at the end.

9: A water element at Sangath.
Photo courtesy: Dinesh Mehta

Architecture embodies emotions. It is a chemistry between the 'conceptual' and the 'perceptual.' Architectural constructs set in motion a dialogue between the conceptual notions, as encoded by the designer while conceiving the space, and its perception, as deciphered by the perceiver guided through the senses of his body as well as his mind. This dialogue succeeds if the communication is mutually concurrent and the comprehension is thorough. Successful architecture manages to bring together these qualities by basing its communication on the most fundamental tenets of mind and matter. When an idea stems from the contextual notions of its time, space and existence, the mental processes of communication, comprehension and perception are implied as inherently intuitive. Whereas in the case of matter, perceived sensorially, the communication is humanly universal and implicitly understood. Together, they mark the complete communication–a wholesome experience integrating the spiritual and the corporeal.

TIMELESS ARCHITECTURE TRADES ON THESE DUALITIES:

–OF TIME AND SPACE

–OF MIND AND MATTER

–OF NOTIONS AND REALITY

–OF THE MICROCOSM AND THE COSMOS

–OF THE 'CONCEPTUAL' AND THE 'PERCEPTUAL'

Glossary

Annapurna: The goddess of sustained nourishment

***arghya*:** the ritual of offering water in the cupped palms to the rising/setting sun, symbolically bringing together water and fire, through reflection of the sun's rays in the water.

Ardhanarishwara: one of the forms of Lord Shiva, depicted as half-man and half-woman, symbolizing the harmonious balance between the extremes and complementarity of the two.

***asana*:** seat. Mythologically each deity had his own specific seat: For example, Lord Brahma used to sit on a lotus, so it was called *padmasana*.

Atman: the soul of an individual or the microcosm, embodying the total essence of the overall entity. It is conceived as the smallest, indivisible part of the individual, similar to the atom, which though minute completely contains all the characteristics of the whole entity.

***bhunga*:** traditional houseform of Kutchchh desert with circular adobe walls and a thatch roof

Brahman: the eternal universe, the cosmos encompassing all existence

Chandra: synonym for the moon, or the moon god.

***chhaja*:** projecting slab, usually inclined over the lintel to protect the opening from sun and rain

***chhatri*:** an umbrella shaped small pavilion meant for relaxation. It is also erected to commemorate the burial of prominent persons.

Dashavatara: the ten incarnations of Lord Vishnu–*matsya* (fish), *kurma* (tortoise), *varaha* (boar), Narsimha (lion-man), Vamana (dwarf), Parashurama, Rama, Krishna, Buddha and Kalki. Reiterating the concept of cyclical time, each incarnation represents one cycle of creation, sustenance and destruction. These ten incarnations also mark the stages of evolution of life on earth.

***diya*:** the ritual lamp lit before the deity to denote respect; it is notionally associative of the ridding of ignorance.

Ganesha Deoli: a small shrine generally at gateways to propitiate Lord Ganesha for the removal of sins.

***garbhagriha*:** the innermost sanctum of a Hindu temple, where the deity is placed, usually an intimate, enclosed and dark space in the shrine.

***goodha mandapa*:** the middle cell of a tripartite zone of the temple consisting of a walled enclosure with cupola and door window openings. This serves as an antechamber for the *garbhagriha*. It is used for intense religious discourses.

***gopuram*:** literally meaning entry to the city, a tall tapering structure, which functions as a gateway, a characteristic feature of South Indian temple precincts.

Jagdish: name for Lord Vishnu

***jharokha*:** a projecting balcony or a window, like a bay window, on the first and upper floors; it is usually a living space extended outwards to relate better to the outdoors yet maintain privacy within.

Kalapurusha: the Puranic scriptures personify the phenomenon of time as embodied by the Kalapurusha. This notion of time, however, was seen to have a definite beginning, denoted by creation; a duration, denoted by sustenance; and an end, denoted by dissolution. After each dissolution, the cycle of creation, sustenance and destruction recurred. Interestingly, this notion of cyclical time is depicted by the representation of Kalapurusha in a circular form, with his feet touching his head.

***kalash*:** mythologically referred to as the vessel that never empties, it signifies abundance, prosperity and well-being.

Kanch-ki-Burj: a small precint within the Udaipur Palace called the palace of glass crystal

***karnakar*:** the *mudra* (gesture) of the hand depicting the ear.

***khanqah*:** place for imparting education and relaxation

***kharashila pitha*:** classical decorative high plinth upon which the edifice is raised. It is accessed by a central flight of stairs.

***kirtimukha*:** a half-lion, half-dragon architectural motif, known as 'the face of glory'

***kum-kum*:** red powder ritualistically applied on the body or object as an auspicious symbol

***kund*:** an artificially made water tank which has descending *ghat*-like steps

***liwan*:** the colonnaded mosque proper, the inner wall of which always faces Mecca. It is here that the priest sits and sermonizes during prayer sessions.

***mahal*:** a local name for a palace or a small part of a palace

Maharana: a great king

***mardana*:** the realm reserved for male members; it is mostly here that the court is held and guests are welcomed.

***marg*:** a local name for pathway or road

***mayur*-arch:** an arch which creates an opening resembling the form of a peacock with outspread plumage (*mayur*–peacock)

***mehrab*:** a niche in the *quibla* wall of the mosque which symbolizes the axis to God

***mulaprasada*:** the circumambulatory space around the central sanctum

***naman*:** the prayer ritual of paying obeisance by the sense of touch. Increased contact with the body is representative of greater respect.

***nritya-mandapa*:** *Nritya* = dance + *mandapa* = pavilion; a dance pavilion which comes as the first hierarchical space in the traditional Hindu temple.

***padma*:** a lotus

***patal lok*:** the nether world, a part of the three mythological worlds of sky, ground and below earth, it denotes the opposite of the celestial.

***pol*:** a residential precinct of traditional living quarters consisting of linear clusters of houses placed in a row; a popular term in Gujarat.

***pradakshina-patha*:** the circumambulatory path

Puranas: One of a class of Hindu sacred writings chiefly from A.D. 300 to A.D. 750 comprising popular myths, legends and other traditional lore.

***quibla* wall:** the wall facing the holiest place for Muslims, 'the Kaaba' in Mecca

Rajyangan: the royal court meant for receiving the dignitaries and the royal entourage.

***rasa*:** the essence; a composite mixture of things–emotions, juices or extracts–used commonly to denote the sense of taste or emotion.

***Ras-lila*:** a depiction of a dance sequence where Lord Krishna is seen dancing individually, yet simultaneously, with many *gopis*, cowherd women of Vraj. This creates an illusion for each *gopi* that He is with her alone.

***rauza*:** a Sufi name for a tomb

***riwaq*:** the arcaded verandah-like space which surrounds and encloses the mosque courtyard to provide contained space within

***sabha mandapa*:** the first cell of the tripartite zoning of a Hindu temple, consisting of column frames and low rise cupola.

***sahak*:** the court enclosed within the surrounding arcades facing the mosque.

Samudra manthana: the mythological churning of the ocean by the gods and demons to retrieve nectar. They wrapped a huge serpent around a mountain placed upon a tortoise to act as a churning rod.

Shesh-naga: an aggrandized form of the king of serpents, the king cobra, mythologically said to be the vehicle of Lord Vishnu.

***shikhara*:** the pyramidal steeple form capping the innermost sanctum of the shrine denoting and establishing the connection to the divine.

***shringar*:** the ritualistic art of adornment of women

Shiv-linga: The depiction of Lord Shiva as a symbolic unification of the male and female reproductive organs, the phallus and the vulva. The female form alludes to the divine mother or nature, seen as the life giver and nurturer, while the male form refers to the primordial masculinity, the omnipotent seed of creation.

silahkhana: a place meant for meetings and for imparting advice

Tandava Nritya: the cosmic dance of Shiva, a dance of destruction. Consisting of aggressive movements and a crescendo of rhythms, the dance is characterized by fury as well as energy.

tirthankaras: Jainism after Lord Mahavir was spread through the words of 24 of his sanctified saints. They are referred to as *tirthankaras* and are revered today as deities.

torana: a Gujarati term for an entrance arch forming a gateway

tulsi: the basil plant, considered holy in the Hindu faith

vaju: the ritual cleansing done before prayers by members of the Islamic faith.

Virupaksha: A form of the lord Vishnu

yagna: a fire ritual which invokes karmic energies to converge on that centre

zenana: a realm totally dedicalted to female members or ladies belonging to the king's harem.

Miniature style painting of the Udai Bilas Palace at Dungarpur.

References

Ambalal, Amit , *Krishna as Shrinathji*—Rajasthani Paintings from Nathdwara Bookwise (India) Pvt. Ltd. & Mapin Publications Pvt. Ltd. Ahmedabad, 1987

Brown, Percy, *Indian Architecture*: (Buddhist and Hindu), D. B. Taraporevala Sons and Co. Bombay, 1983

Ecole de Beaux-Arts, *Architecture in India*, Electa Moniteur, Paris, 1985-86

Goswamy, B.N. and Fischer, Eberhard, *Pahari Masters*, Oxford University Press (India), 1997

Herdeg, Clause, *Formal Structures in Indian Architecture*, Ithaca, 1997

Jain-Neubauer, Jutta, *The Stepwells of Gujarat: In Art-Historical Perspective*, New Delhi, Abhinav Publications, 1981

Kagal, Carmen, (Ed.) *Vistara: The Architecture of India*, The Festival of India, 1986

De Koning, Krijn, *Inside Outside*, Rotterdam, NAi Publishers, 2000

Lane-Smith, Ron, *Temple Cave Design: The Foundation of a Tradition*, Vastu-Shilpa Foundation, Ahmedabad, 1996

Mansukhani, Raju, Dipti Khera, *The City within a City*–Volume 1, Jagmandir on Lake Pichola Maharana Mewar Charitable Foundation, 2002

Meininger, Irmgard, *City Palace of Udaipur*, D.K.Printworld (P)Ltd.,2000

Michell, George, *Royal Palaces of India*, Thames and Hudson Ltd., London, 1994

Stierlin, Henry, *Hindu India: From Khajuraho to the Temple City of Madurai*, Benedikt Taschen Verlag GmbH, 1998

Tadgell, Christopher, *History of Architecture in India*, Viking Penguin Books (India) Ltd., 1990